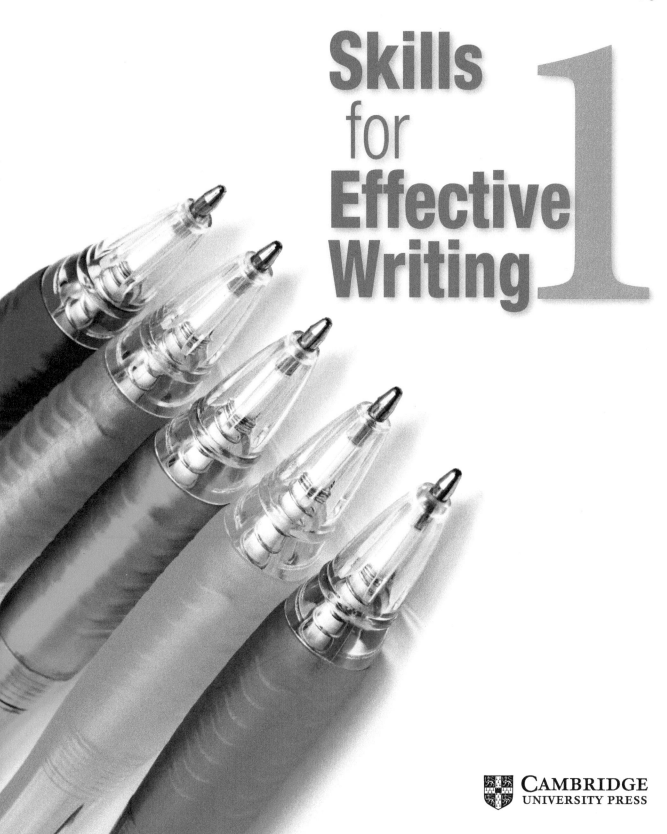

Skills for Effective Writing 1

CAMBRIDGE UNIVERSITY PRESS

CAMBRIDGE UNIVERSITY PRESS
Cambridge, New York, Melbourne, Madrid, Cape Town,
Singapore, São Paulo, Delhi, Mexico City

Cambridge University Press
32 Avenue of the Americas, New York, NY 10013-2473, USA

www.cambridge.org
Information on this title: www.cambridge.org/9781107684348

First published 2013

Printed in the United States of America

A catalog record for this publication is available from the British Library.

ISBN 978-1-107-68434-8 Student's Book

The publisher wishes to acknowledge the contributions of the following writers:
Neta Simpkins Cahill, Susan Hills, Hilary Hodge, Elizabeth Iannotti,
Robyn Brinks Lockwood, and Kathryn O'Dell.

Art direction, book design, cover design, editorial management, layout services,
and photo research: Hyphen S.A.

Cover image: ©Ingmar Bjork/Shutterstock.com

Photography: 2 ©Poznyakov/Shutterstock.com; 6 ©Helder Alemida/Shutterstock.com;
10 ©Blend Images/Superstock; 14 ©artur gabrysiak/Shutterstock.com; 18 ©Stephen
Coburn/Shutterstock.com; 22 ©art&design/Shutterstock.com; 26 ©Jose AS Reyes/
Shutterstock.com; 30 ©Andresr/Shutterstock.com; 34 ©Stanislav Komogorov/
Shutterstock.com; 38 ©Jakez/Shutterstock.com; 42 ©iStockphoto.com/arekmalang;
46 ©Supri Suharjoto/Shutterstock.com; 50 ©Deklofenak/Shutterstock.com;
54 ©mikeldray/Shutterstock.com; 58 ©iStockphoto.com/Ashrafov; 62 ©Anna
Hoychuk/Shutterstock.com; 66 ©Bobo Ling/Shutterstock.com; 70 ©iStockphoto.com/
RapidEye; 74 ©Monkey Business Images/Shutterstock.com; 78 ©iStockphoto.com/
nuno; 82 ©iStockphoto.com/teekid; 86 ©Monkey Business Images/Shutterstock.com;
90 ©StockLite/Shutterstock.com; 94 ©1971yes/Shutterstock.com; 98 ©RoJo Images/
Shutterstock.com; 102 ©erwinova/Shutterstock.com; 106 ©ampyang/Shutterstock.
com; 110 ©iStockphoto.com/kirstypargeter; 114 ©Yanik Chauvin/Shutterstock.com;
118 ©Konstantin Yolshin/Shutterstock.com; 122 ©Tomasz Trojanowski; 126 ©Goodluz/
Shutterstock.com; 130 ©Carolina K. Smith M.D./Shutterstock.com

Skills for Effective Writing 1

CAMBRIDGE

Contents

Discrete writing skills, such as creating topic sentences and recognizing irrelevant information, are critical for good writers. This 4-level series teaches these skills and offers extensive practice opportunities.

SKILL PRESENTATION

Each unit teaches a single discrete writing skill, helping students focus their attention on developing the skill fully.

OVER TO YOU

Following instruction, students are eased into the skill's application, facilitating their understanding of exactly how each skill works.

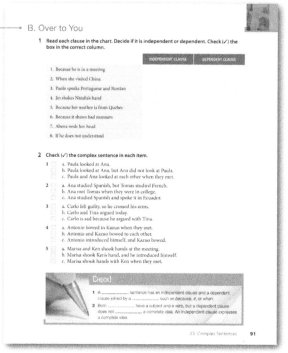

When students master these skills, all of their writing improves. This allows teachers to focus their time and feedback on the content of student work.

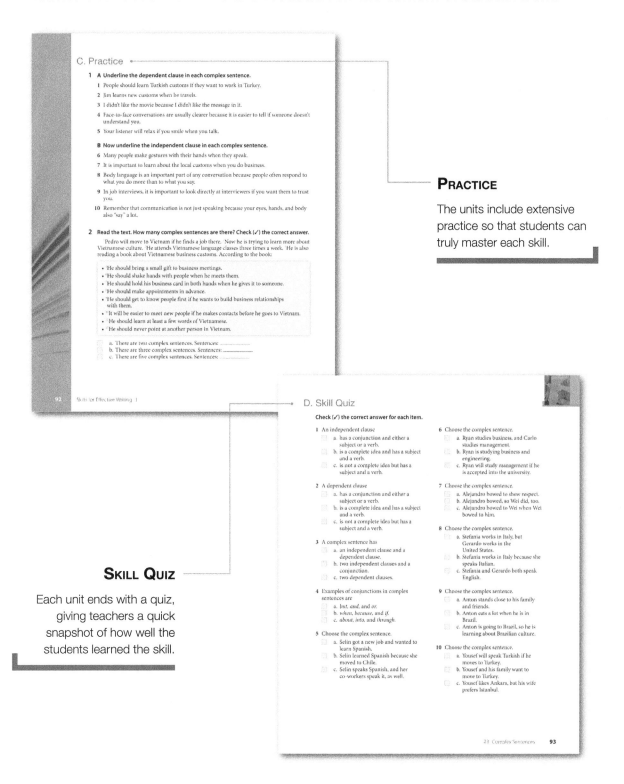

C. Practice

1 A Underline the dependent clause in each complex sentence.

1 People should learn Turkish customs if they want to work in Turkey.

2 Jim learns new customs when he travels.

3 I didn't like the movie because I didn't like the message in it.

4 Face-to-face conversations are usually clearer because it is easier to tell if someone doesn't understand you.

5 Your listener will relax if you smile when you talk.

B Now underline the independent clause in each complex sentence.

6 Many people make gestures with their hands when they speak.

7 It is important to learn about the local customs when you do business.

8 Body language is an important part of any conversation because people often respond to what you do more than to what you say.

9 In job interviews, it is important to look directly at interviewers if you want them to trust you.

10 Remember that communication is not just speaking because your eyes, hands, and body also "say" a lot.

2 Read the text. How many complex sentences are there? Check (✓) the correct answer.

¹Pedro will move to Vietnam if he finds a job there. ²Now he is trying to learn more about Vietnamese culture. ³He attends Vietnamese language classes three times a week. ⁴He is also reading a book about Vietnamese business customs. According to the book:

- ⁵He should bring a small gift to business meetings.
- ⁶He should shake hands with people when he meets them.
- ⁷He should hold his business card in both hands when he gives it to someone.
- ⁸He should make appointments in advance.
- ⁹He should get to know people first if he wants to build business relationships with them.
- ¹⁰It will be easier to meet new people if he makes contacts before he goes to Vietnam.
- ¹¹He should learn at least a few words of Vietnamese.
- ¹²He should never point at another person in Vietnam.

☐ a. There are two complex sentences. Sentences: _____

☐ b. There are three complex sentences. Sentences: _____

☐ c. There are five complex sentences. Sentences: _____

92 Skills for Effective Writing 1

PRACTICE

The units include extensive practice so that students can truly master each skill.

SKILL QUIZ

Each unit ends with a quiz, giving teachers a quick snapshot of how well the students learned the skill.

D. Skill Quiz

Check (✓) the correct answer for each item.

1 An independent clause

☐ a. has a conjunction and either a subject or a verb.

☐ b. is a complete idea and has a subject and a verb.

☐ c. is not a complete idea but has a subject and a verb.

2 A dependent clause

☐ a. has a conjunction and either a subject or a verb.

☐ b. is a complete idea and has a subject and a verb.

☐ c. is not a complete idea but has a subject and a verb.

3 A complex sentence has

☐ a. an independent clause and a dependent clause.

☐ b. two independent clauses and a conjunction.

☐ c. two dependent clauses.

4 Examples of conjunctions in complex sentences are

☐ a. *but, and,* and *or.*

☐ b. *when, because,* and *if.*

☐ c. *about, into,* and *through.*

5 Choose the complex sentence.

☐ a. Selin got a new job and wanted to learn Spanish.

☐ b. Selin learned Spanish because she moved to Chile.

☐ c. Selin speaks Spanish, and her co-workers speak it, as well.

6 Choose the complex sentence.

☐ a. Ryan studies business, and Carlo studies management.

☐ b. Ryan is studying business and engineering.

☐ c. Ryan will study management if he is accepted into the university.

7 Choose the complex sentence.

☐ a. Alejandro bowed to show respect.

☐ b. Alejandro bowed, so Wei did, too.

☐ c. Alejandro bowed to Wei when Wei bowed to him.

8 Choose the complex sentence.

☐ a. Stefania works in Italy, but Gerardo works in the United States.

☐ b. Stefania works in Italy because she speaks Italian.

☐ c. Stefania and Gerardo both speak English.

9 Choose the complex sentence.

☐ a. Anton stands close to his family and friends.

☐ b. Anton eats a lot when he is in Brazil.

☐ c. Anton is going to Brazil, so he is learning about Brazilian culture.

10 Choose the complex sentence.

☐ a. Yousef will speak Turkish if he moves to Turkey.

☐ b. Yousef and his family want to move to Turkey.

☐ c. Yousef likes Ankara, but his wife prefers Istanbul.

23 Complex Sentences   93

PERSONAL INFORMATION

Words, Sentences, and Paragraphs

CONNECTING TO THE THEME

Are you outgoing or shy?

When you meet people, do you	**A** talk about your goals and interests?	**B** ask about them?
When you are in a group, do you	**A** talk the most?	**B** talk the least?
In essays about yourself, do you	**A** have a lot to say?	**B** feel uncomfortable writing about yourself?

Mostly As: outgoing. Mostly Bs: shy.

A. Skill Presentation

Letters make **words**. Most words use small letters.

> teacher, family, good, write

Some words use **capital letters** and small letters together.

> Professor Garcia, State University

A **sentence** always begins with a capital letter. A sentence also has **one space** between two words. Finally, a sentence usually ends with a **period**.

my essay is about me. ✗	My essay is about me. ✓
Myessayisaboutme. ✗	My essay is about me. ✓
My essay is about me ✗	My essay is about me. ✓

Sentences make **paragraphs**. It is important to write paragraphs correctly. A paragraph is about one idea.

In the paragraph below, the sentences *My teacher liked it* and *Maybe I will get a good grade* are about the same idea. The sentence *I like shopping* is not about the same idea as the other sentences. It shouldn't be used.

> I wrote my essay. My teacher liked it. ~~I like shopping~~. Maybe I will get a good grade.

The first line of a paragraph is **indented**. To indent, type about five spaces before the first word. A paragraph is not a list of sentences. At the end of a sentence, type a space. Then begin the next sentence.

I wrote my essay. My teacher liked it. Maybe I will get a good grade. ✗	I wrote my essay. My teacher liked it. Maybe I will get a good grade. ✓

B. Over to You

1 Read the three paragraphs. Check (✓) the correct paragraph.

☐ **1** Today was our first class. We met our instructor. She told us about herself.

☐ **2** Today was our first class.We met our instructor. She told us about herself.

☐ **3** Today was our first class. We met our
instructor. She told us about herself.

2 Correct the sentences and paragraphs.

1 goodessaysareinteresting

_____

2 doctor Goodrich teaches at harvard university

_____

3 My sister read my essay

_____

4 I got a good grade today.
The teacher liked my essay.
I wrote it very carefully.

_____

_____

5 I want to be a doctor I am taking science and math courses I hope to get good grades.

_____

_____

6 My English teacher helped me a lot. She worked with me after class.
She helped me apply to college.

_____

_____

CHECK!

1 Sentences are groups of _____. Sentences begin with a capital
letter and end with a _____. There is one _____ between
the words.

2 _____ are groups of sentences about _____ idea.
Remember to _____ paragraphs.

C. Practice

1 Read each sentence and paragraph in the chart. Decide if they are correct or incorrect. Check (✓) the box in the correct column.

	CORRECT SENTENCE	CORRECT PARAGRAPH	NOT CORRECT
1. Today was our first class. We met our instructor. She told us about herself.			
2. That is my instructor.			
3. I like this essay. I think it is very good. It is very original.			
4. I planned my essay carefully. I wrote down a lot of ideas. I chose the best ideas. Then I started writing.			
5. The nursing program is very good			
6. malena wrote her personal essay. it took three hours. she needed more time.			
7. I play tennis everySaturday.			
8. I was very busy in high school I played basketball I got very good grades I also worked after school every day			

2 Match each paragraph (A–D) with the correct description (1–4).

__ **1** No mistakes   __ **3** Not a paragraph

__ **2** Mistakes with spaces   __ **4** Mistakes with capital letters

A   Iaminterestedinhistory. Iliketoreadbooksaboutimportantpeopleandeventsfromthepast. Ialsowatchhistoricalmovies. SometimesIgotolectures. IwanttolearnasmuchasIcan.

B   I am interested in history. I like to read books about important people and events from the past. I also watch historical movies. Sometimes I go to lectures. I want to learn as much as I can.

C   I am interested in history. I like to read books about important people and events from the past.
I also watch historical movies.
Sometimes I go to lectures.
I want to learn as much as I can.

D   I am interested in history. i like to read books about important people and events from the past. i also watch historical movies. sometimes i go to lectures. i want to learn as much as I can.

D. Skill Quiz

Check (✓) the correct answer for each item.

1 A sentence has
    ☐ a. words and spaces.
    ☐ b. indentations and periods.
    ☐ c. only capital letters.

2 A sentence has
    ☐ a. a period.
    ☐ b. a capital letter.
    ☐ c. a period and a capital letter.

3 A paragraph
    ☐ a. is a list.
    ☐ b. has an indentation.
    ☐ c. has one or two words.

4 A paragraph is
    ☐ a. about one idea.
    ☐ b. about many ideas.
    ☐ c. the same thing as a sentence.

5 *my bedroom is very messy*
This sentence needs
    ☐ a. a period.
    ☐ b. a capital letter.
    ☐ c. a period and a capital letter.

6 *Myteacherisbusy.*
This sentence needs
    ☐ a. a period.
    ☐ b. a capital letter.
    ☐ c. spaces between words.

7 *I buy lots of technology. I have two cell phones. I have a laptop. I also have an iPad. My friends say I don't need anything else.*
This paragraph
    ☐ a. needs to be indented.
    ☐ b. is correct.
    ☐ c. needs spaces between sentences.

8 *my favorite subject is math. i enjoy my classes. the math classes are difficult. my teacher helps me.*
This paragraph needs
    ☐ a. more ideas.
    ☐ b. more spaces between words.
    ☐ c. sentences that start with capital letters.

9 *I am interested in sports and health.I am good at working with people.I hope to get a job doing both.I would like to be a physical therapist.*
This paragraph needs
    ☐ a. a list of sentences.
    ☐ b. more capital letters.
    ☐ c. one space between each sentence.

10 *I amwriting anessay. The teacher gave me some examples. I have some goodideas towriteabout. Myessay willbe interesting.*
This paragraph needs
    ☐ a. all capital letters.
    ☐ b. spaces between words.
    ☐ c. all capital letters and spaces between words.

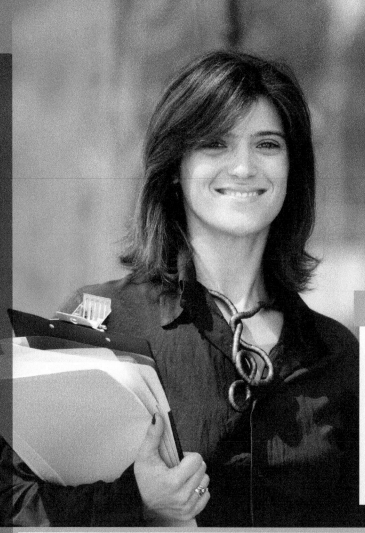

SCHEDULES

CONNECTING TO THE THEME

Are you organized?

I always get to class
   A early.   **B** on time.   **C** late.

Do you make a plan of what you have to do?
   A always   **B** sometimes   **C** never

Can you always find your books, keys, and cell phone when you need them?
   A yes   **B** usually   **C** no

Mostly As: organized. Mostly Bs: sometimes organized. Mostly Cs: disorganized.

A. Skill Presentation

A statement is a sentence that **gives information**. A statement always ends with a period.

   My next class is at noon.

If the sentence **asks for information**, it is a question. Many questions use a **question word**. Some question words are *who*, *what*, *where*, *when*, *why*, *how*, *do*, and *did*. A question ends with a **question mark**.

   When is your next class?

There are other words that can begin questions, like *are*, *is*, *was*, and *were*. If you use one of these words at the beginning of a sentence, put a question mark at the end.

There is also punctuation used in the middle of sentences, called **commas**. Use a comma when you write dates. The comma goes between the day and the year.

   School starts on September 1, 2013.

Use commas when you write lists that have three or more items. Put a comma after each item except for the last item. Remember to put a comma before the word *and*.

   Ivan is taking math, science, and history classes.

B. Over to You

1 Read the sentences. Check (✓) *Statement* or *Question*. Add a period or question mark at the end of each sentence.

Statement	Question	
☐	☐	**1** When are you leaving for class ___
☐	☐	**2** There are 15 people in my class ___
☐	☐	**3** Do you have a math test today ___
☐	☐	**4** How many classes are you taking ___
☐	☐	**5** The English class is in Hudson Hall ___
☐	☐	**6** The next meeting is on Tuesday ___
☐	☐	**7** Are you sure the class starts at 10:00 a.m. ___
☐	☐	**8** I have an unusual schedule this week ___
☐	☐	**9** What are you doing after class ___
☐	☐	**10** At 3:30 p.m. my class is over ___

2 Read the sentences and add commas where necessary. If no comma is needed, leave it blank.

1 Most students take English math and science.

2 I started school on June 25 2012.

3 I go to the library on Monday Tuesday and Wednesday nights.

4 School was over on April 7 2012.

5 I studied English with Dr. Lee Ms. Bunting and Mr. Johns.

6 The language lab has computers printers and copy machines.

7 We meet for breakfast coffee and dessert.

8 Fall classes began on September 15 2013.

9 Juan went to school in Missouri Colorado and California.

10 My favorite subjects are English health and history.

CHECK!

1 A _____ is a sentence that gives _____. Use a _____ to end a statement.

2 A _____ is a sentence that _____ for information. Use a _____ _____ to end a question.

3 Commas go in the _____ of sentences. Use a comma with _____ and in lists with _____ or more items.

C. Practice

1 Read each sentence in the chart. Decide if the punctuation (period, question mark, commas) in each sentence is correct. Check (✓) the box in the correct column.

	CORRECT PUNCTUATION	INCORRECT PUNCTUATION
1. I am taking four classes.		
2. Are you taking a reading class.		
3. My favorite class is history?		
4. Who is your favorite teacher?		
5. My friend finished school on May 15, 2013.		
6. The computer lab opens on October, 3 2013.		
7. The lab is open on Tuesday, Wednesday and Thursday.		
8. There are no classes in June, July, and August.		
9. What are you doing at noon.		
10. Registration begins next October?		
11. Are you taking three classes?		
12. The math class is difficult.		

2 Read the statements or questions. Add the correct punctuation (period, question mark, commas). If no punctuation is needed, leave it blank.

1 Who is your teacher ___

2 My vacation starts on June ___ 10 ___ 2013 ___

3 Do you like ___ your English class ___

4 My favorite classes are English ___ math ___ and music ___

5 My science class ___ is difficult ___

6 I am taking math ___

7 The computer labs are in Building ___ A ___ Building C ___ and Building D ___

8 Where ___ is your next class ___

9 My next class is on Monday ___

10 School ended on May ___ 31 ___ 2013 ___

D. Skill Quiz

Check (✓) the correct answer for each item.

1 A sentence that asks for information ends with a

◻ a. comma.
◻ b. period.
◻ c. question mark.

2 A sentence that gives information ends with a

◻ a. comma.
◻ b. period.
◻ c. question mark.

3 A sentence that gives a day and year always uses a

◻ a. comma.
◻ b. period.
◻ c. question mark.

4 Use a comma when you list

◻ a. one item.
◻ b. two items.
◻ c. three or more items.

5 Which list has commas in the correct place?

◻ a. Monday Wednesday and Friday
◻ b. Monday, Wednesday, and Friday
◻ c. Monday, Wednesday, and, Friday

6 *The exam is from 10:00 a.m. to 11:00 a.m. on September 27, 2010?*
This sentence is incorrect because

◻ a. there should not be a comma after *27*.
◻ b. there should be a period at the end.
◻ c. there should be a comma before *to*.

7 *She is my favorite teacher because she is fun interesting, and smart.*
This sentence is incorrect because

◻ a. there should be a comma after *and*.
◻ b. there should be a comma after *fun*.
◻ c. there should not be a comma after *interesting*.

8 Which sentence is correct?

◻ a. Do you like that class.
◻ b. It is my favorite class?
◻ c. When did you go to that class?

9 Choose the correct punctuation to end this sentence: *Who are you meeting* ___

◻ a. ,
◻ b. .
◻ c. ?

10 Choose the correct punctuation to end this sentence: *I am taking three classes* ___

◻ a. ,
◻ b. .
◻ c. ?

3

Capitalization Rules 1

GADGETS

CONNECTING TO THE THEME

Do you use gadgets to help you study?

I look up words
  A in a dictionary.   **B** on my cell phone.   **C** on an electronic dictionary.

I take notes
  A in a notebook.   **B** on my laptop.   **C** on my tablet with a digital pen.

I check my e-mail
  A at a computer lab.   **B** on my laptop.   **C** on my cell phone.

Mostly As: you do not buy many gadgets. Mostly Bs: you like to own some gadgets. Mostly Cs: you are hooked on owning gadgets.

A. Skill Presentation

To **capitalize** a letter is to make it a capital. **Capital letters** are usually bigger than lowercase letters. When you write, always capitalize the first letter of the first word in a sentence.

> They bought new cameras.

> She bought a new laptop.

There are some words you always capitalize. Always capitalize the pronoun *I*.

> John says that **I** should buy the basic model of the cell phone.

Also, always capitalize the days of the week: *Sunday, Monday, Tuesday, Wednesday, Thursday, Friday,* and *Saturday*.

> My friend and I go to the computer lab every Saturday.

B. Over to You

1 Read the three sentences. Check (✓) the correct sentence.

☐ **1** today i am going to buy a new cell phone.

☐ **2** today I am going to buy a new cell phone.

☐ **3** Today I am going to buy a new cell phone.

2 Read each sentence in the chart. If the sentence is not correct, which rule does it break? Check (✓) the box in the correct column.

	CAPITALIZE THE FIRST LETTER OF THE FIRST WORD IN A SENTENCE.	CAPITALIZE THE PRONOUN *I*.	CAPITALIZE THE DAYS OF THE WEEK.	THE SENTENCE IS CORRECT.
1. he is going to buy an electronic dictionary.				
2. She and i bought a new wireless printer on Tuesday.				
3. I only buy electronics online.				
4. My friend said i should buy a used cell phone.				
5. they want cell phones with cameras.				
6. The computer lab is closed.				
7. She sent me an e-mail on Sunday night.				
8. my friends like to send text messages.				
9. My sister and i both have new laptops.				
10. I think I will buy a cell phone on saturday.				

CHECK!

1 Always capitalize the _____ letter of the first word in a _____ .

2 Always _____ the pronoun _____ .

3 Always capitalize the _____ of the week.

C. Practice

1 **Read the paragraphs. How many mistakes with capitalization are there in each paragraph? Circle them and check (✓) the correct answer.**

1   Julio and i are at the computer store. We are comparing new and used computers. the new computers are very high quality. They work very well. They have many great features, too. Most of the new computers have built-in webcams. the used computers are lower quality. i think Julio should buy a new computer. he agrees.

☐   a. There are two mistakes with capitalization.
☐   b. There are five mistakes with capitalization.
☐   c. There are seven mistakes with capitalization.

2   My math professor and i are meeting on tuesday. we are going to discuss my grades in the course. he wants to talk to me over webcam, but i like to meet in person.

☐   a. There are five mistakes with capitalization.
☐   b. There are six mistakes with capitalization.
☐   c. There are seven mistakes with capitalization.

3   i use my new cell phone for everything. For example, i e-mail my friends and family. i take pictures of my friends on it, too. i also look up words in an online dictionary. sometimes, i even video call my family on saturdays using it.

☐   a. There are six mistakes with capitalization.
☐   b. There are seven mistakes with capitalization.
☐   c. There are eight mistakes with capitalization.

2 **Circle the letters that should be capital.**

1 the new model of this cell phone is expensive. it does a lot of things.

2 i check my e-mail on my cell phone.

3 i listen to music on my cell phone when i'm on the train.

4 i bought a used laptop on monday. the new ones were too expensive.

5 my sister has a tablet.

6 people use their cellphones to send text messages.

7 sometimes sending a text message is easier than talking.

8 my dad is buying me a new tablet for my birthday.

9 mom and i are in a cell-phone store.

10 avery uses the camera on his cellphone to take pictures of his friends.

D. Skill Quiz

Check (✓) the correct answer for each item.

1 Capital letters
   - ☐ a. are usually smaller than lowercase letters.
   - ☐ b. are usually the same size as lowercase letters.
   - ☐ c. are often bigger than lowercase letters.

2 The first letter in a sentence is always
   - ☐ a. a pronoun.
   - ☐ b. capitalized.
   - ☐ c. important.

3 Always capitalize
   - ☐ a. the pronoun *I*.
   - ☐ b. the word *and*.
   - ☐ c. every word in a sentence.

4 Choose the sentence with the correct capitalization.
   - ☐ a. Julietta and i are going to the mall.
   - ☐ b. Julietta and I are going to the mall.
   - ☐ c. julietta and I are going to the mall.

5 Choose the sentence with the correct capitalization.
   - ☐ a. i use my laptop when i give presentations.
   - ☐ b. I use my laptop when i give presentations.
   - ☐ c. I use my laptop when I give presentations.

6 Choose the sentence with the correct capitalization.
   - ☐ a. He is going to a used electronics store on Wednesday.
   - ☐ b. He is going to a used electronics store on wednesday.
   - ☐ c. he is going To a used electronics store on Wednesday.

7 Choose the sentence with the correct capitalization.
   - ☐ a. Chen sent Li a text message to make plans.
   - ☐ b. chen sent Li a text message to make plans.
   - ☐ c. Chen sent Li a Text Message to make plans.

8 Choose the sentence with the correct capitalization.
   - ☐ a. The new model of the cell phone is available in orange.
   - ☐ b. the new model of the cell phone is available in orange.
   - ☐ c. The new model of the cell phone Is available In orange.

9 *my teacher says it is important to bring our laptops to class.*
   - ☐ a. The letter *m* in *my* needs to be capitalized in this sentence.
   - ☐ b. The letter *i* in *it* needs to be capitalized in this sentence.
   - ☐ c. This sentence is correct.

10 *Maria and i are comparing new and used cell phones.*
   - ☐ a. The *m* in *Maria* does not need to be capitalized in this sentence.
   - ☐ b. The pronoun *i* needs to be capitalized in this sentence.
   - ☐ c. This sentence is correct.

CONNECTING TO THE THEME

What is your working style?

Working in a group
    A makes you nervous.   **B** can take time.   **C** gets the job done.

Can you plan and make a decision with others?
    A not usually   **B** it depends   **C** always

Are you comfortable asking others for help and advice?
    A not at all   **B** if I know them   **C** absolutely

Mostly As: you prefer to lead and work alone. Mostly Bs: you like being part of a team, but like to lead sometimes. Mostly Cs: you like to work with other people and be told what to do.

A. Skill Presentation

Claudia, manager, sister

Bangkok, hall, office

A noun is a **person**, **thing**, **place**, or **idea**.

folder, printer, copy machine

information, time, knowledge

Most nouns can be **singular** (only one) or **plural** (more than one). Plural nouns usually end in -*s*.

| **SINGULAR** | manager | folder | meeting |
| **PLURAL** | managers | folders | meetings |

However, not all plural nouns end in -*s*. A plural noun that does not end in -*s* is called an **irregular plural**.

| **SINGULAR** | woman | man | person |
| **PLURAL** | women | men | people |

When you write nouns, be sure to use the correct plural form – either regular or irregular.

B. Over to You

1 Read the sentences and check (✓) the nouns.

1 The meeting is at exactly 4:30 p.m.

- ☐ a. meeting
- ☐ b. is
- ☐ c. exactly

2 There are almost no supplies left.

- ☐ a. are
- ☐ b. almost
- ☐ c. supplies

3 The team was talking.

- ☐ a. team
- ☐ b. was
- ☐ c. talking

4 Simon speaks slowly.

- ☐ a. Simon
- ☐ b. speaks
- ☐ c. slowly

5 Where is my folder?

- ☐ a. where
- ☐ b. my
- ☐ c. folder

6 Look for some paper, please.

- ☐ a. some
- ☐ b. paper
- ☐ c. please

2 Read each sentence in the chart. Which type of noun is in bold in each sentence: a person, a place, a thing, or an idea? Check (✓) the box in the correct column.

	PERSON	PLACE	THING	IDEA
1. The **manager** is very friendly.				
2. This **city** is growing slowly.				
3. The **meetings** start at 3:00 p.m.				
4. The **report** was 20 pages long.				
5. The team welcomed the new **employee** to the company.				
6. People spend a lot of **money** on work supplies.				
7. The **printer** is out of ink again.				
8. **New York** is a big financial center.				
9. New employees often experience some **stress**.				
10. We will have a meeting at the **office** tomorrow.				

CHECK!

1 A noun is a word for a _____, place, thing, or _____.

2 Most nouns are either _____ (only one) or _____ (more than one). Plural nouns usually _____ in -*s*.

C. Practice

1 Read each sentence in the chart. Decide if the noun in bold in each sentence is singular, regular plural, or irregular plural. Check (✓) the box in the correct column.

	SINGULAR	REGULAR PLURAL	IRREGULAR PLURAL
1. All three **reports** were very well done.			
2. The company **party** was interrupted by rain.			
3. We need **pencils**. We only have pens.			
4. The **women** gave a presentation together at the conference.			
5. The **managers** spend a lot of time in meetings.			
6. Please introduce us to the new **manager**.			
7. Are all the printer supplies kept in one **place**?			
8. I saw several **folders** next to the copy machine.			
9. The manager will introduce our **teams** at the conference.			
10. The **people** from the company met the new employees.			

2 Circle the nouns in each sentence.

1 My boss wants a copy of the report.

2 The workers all like their manager.

3 We need notebooks, pens, and pencils.

4 Those two men run the company.

5 There aren't many people at the meeting today.

6 My printer and copy machine are not working.

7 I couldn't find the folder or the e-mail.

8 Claudia is the manager of this office.

9 Marlee is being transferred to our Bangkok store.

10 I do not have the information to complete the report.

D. Skill Quiz

Check (✓) the correct answer for each item.

1 What is a noun?
- [ ] a. a person, a place, a color, or an idea
- [ ] b. a person, a place, a thing, or an idea
- [ ] c. a person, an action, a thing, or an idea

2 *Building*, *India*, and *office* are
- [ ] a. people.
- [ ] b. places.
- [ ] c. ideas.

3 Plural nouns that do not end in *-s* are
- [ ] a. normal.
- [ ] b. regular.
- [ ] c. irregular.

4 When you write, use
- [ ] a. the correct plural form of the noun.
- [ ] b. only nouns that are regular.
- [ ] c. singular nouns instead of plural nouns.

5 *The <u>manager</u> asked for a meeting after work.*
The underlined noun is
- [ ] a. a person.
- [ ] b. a place.
- [ ] c. an idea.

6 *<u>Time</u> passes quickly when work is fun.*
The underlined noun is
- [ ] a. a person.
- [ ] b. a place.
- [ ] c. an idea.

7 *The <u>people</u> in that company were not happy with their managers.*
The underlined noun is
- [ ] a. singular.
- [ ] b. regular plural.
- [ ] c. irregular plural.

8 *We had too many <u>meetings</u> at work last week.*
The underlined noun is
- [ ] a. singular.
- [ ] b. regular plural.
- [ ] c. irregular plural.

9 *The report Robert wrote about New York is almost finished.*
The noun that names a thing is
- [ ] a. report.
- [ ] b. Robert.
- [ ] c. New York.

10 *The supplies are next to the copy machine in the hall.*
The noun that names a place is
- [ ] a. supplies.
- [ ] b. copy machine.
- [ ] c. hall.

SKILLS AND QUALITIES FOR SUCCESS

CONNECTING TO THE THEME

How ambitious are you?

Yes	No	I work hard at school.
Yes	No	I am organized.
Yes	No	I complete work on time.
Yes	No	I get things done faster than others.
Yes	No	I have clear goals.
Yes	No	I know when to ask for help.

Mostly Yes: ambitious. Mostly No: not so ambitious.

A. Skill Presentation

When you write, it is important to use verbs correctly. It helps your reader understand what is happening. In statements, **nouns** come before **verbs**.

NOUN   **VERB**
Ms. Franklin teaches English.

Most verbs express action. These are called **action verbs**. They say what someone or something does. Some action verbs are *ask*, *find*, and *study*.

Her brother works very long hours.

There are other verbs that do not express action. These are called **non-action** verbs. This kind of verb can show that something belongs to someone.

Mia has goals.   The verb *has* shows us that the goals belong to Mia.

This kind of verb can also help describe a quality.

Emory is intelligent.   The verb *is* shows us that *intelligent* describes Emory.

Finally, this kind of verb can express a feeling.

Dino loves his job.   The verb *love* tells us how Dino feels about his job.

B. Over to You

1 **Read the paragraph. Decide if the verbs in bold express action. Write each verb in the correct column of the chart.**

Larry **is** a good student. He **likes** school. He **asks** his teacher questions. He **has** a lot of homework, and he always **completes** his work on time. He **works** hard, and he **studies** every night. He **feels** successful.

VERBS THAT EXPRESS ACTION	VERBS THAT DO NOT EXPRESS ACTION

2 **Read the paragraphs. How many verbs are there in each paragraph? Circle them and check (✓) the correct answer.**

1   Rafael works at a hospital. He is very busy. He helps the doctors and nurses. He also finds new employees. He needs a new assistant. He wants an ambitious person for this job.

    ☐ a. There are four verbs in this paragraph.
    ☐ b. There are six verbs in this paragraph.
    ☐ c. There are seven verbs in this paragraph.

2   Loretta is unemployed. She is a professional, and she wants a job at a bank. She looks on the Internet for jobs. She sees a job posting on Globo Bank's website. She sends her résumé to the bank. She hopes they call her soon.

    ☐ a. There are four verbs in this paragraph.
    ☐ b. There are six verbs in this paragraph.
    ☐ c. There are eight verbs in this paragraph.

CHECK!

1 In English, verbs come after _____ in statements.

2 Most verbs express _____, but there are some verbs that do _____ express action.

C. Practice

1 Read each sentence in the chart. Decide if the verb is in the correct place. Check (✓) the box in the correct column.

	CORRECT	NOT CORRECT
1. Loretta's goal to work is at the hospital. She hopes to get a job there soon.		
2. Lorna is looking for a job. Right now she is unemployed.		
3. There is a website with useful information about jobs. It Mario helped find a new career.		
4. Mario to work wants with nurses and doctors. He likes to work with professionals.		
5. Took my brother a course to learn how to be an administrative assistant. He gained some excellent skills.		
6. David is very ambitious. He always tries to do better at work so he can get a promotion or raise.		
7. Many enjoy people social networking. They like to stay in touch with friends.		
8. An employer saw at a small business Sophie's information online.		
9. My daughter updated her profile online. She added new information about her interests.		
10. Sophie has an interview next week for a job at the small business.		

2 Make sentences. Write the words in the correct order. Don't forget to add a period.

1 are | social | networking sites | useful

_____

2 work | they | hard

_____

3 a lot | studies | Isobel

_____

4 profile | is | Ryan's | online

_____

5 together | work | we | well

_____

6 ambitious | they | are

_____

D. Skill Quiz

Check (✓) the correct answer for each item.

1 What does an action verb do?
   - ☐ a. tells what a person does
   - ☐ b. shows who is doing the action
   - ☐ c. describes a person's qualities

2 Which verbs do not express action?
   - ☐ a. *go* and *ask*
   - ☐ b. *work* and *study*
   - ☐ c. *have* and *be*

3 In statements, a verb
   - ☐ a. is the first word in a sentence.
   - ☐ b. is not necessary.
   - ☐ c. comes after a noun.

4 *Wendy is ambitious and hardworking.*
   What is the verb in this sentence?
   - ☐ a. is
   - ☐ b. ambitious
   - ☐ c. hardworking

5 *She works at a hospital.*
   What is the verb in this sentence?
   - ☐ a. She
   - ☐ b. works
   - ☐ c. hospital

6 *Mr. Ito teaches a difficult course.*
   What is the verb in this sentence?
   - ☐ a. Mr. Ito
   - ☐ b. teaches
   - ☐ c. course

7 *I have a lot of goals for the future.*
   What is the verb in this sentence?
   - ☐ a. have
   - ☐ b. goals
   - ☐ c. future

8 Choose the verb that correctly completes
   this sentence: *We ___ our employees
   by phone.*
   - ☐ a. are
   - ☐ b. contact
   - ☐ c. use

9 Choose the verb that correctly completes
   this sentence: *Jacob ___ a hardworking
   student.*
   - ☐ a. is
   - ☐ b. sells
   - ☐ c. studies

10 Choose the verb that correctly completes
   this sentence: *I ___ a new job.*
   - ☐ a. am
   - ☐ b. read
   - ☐ c. want

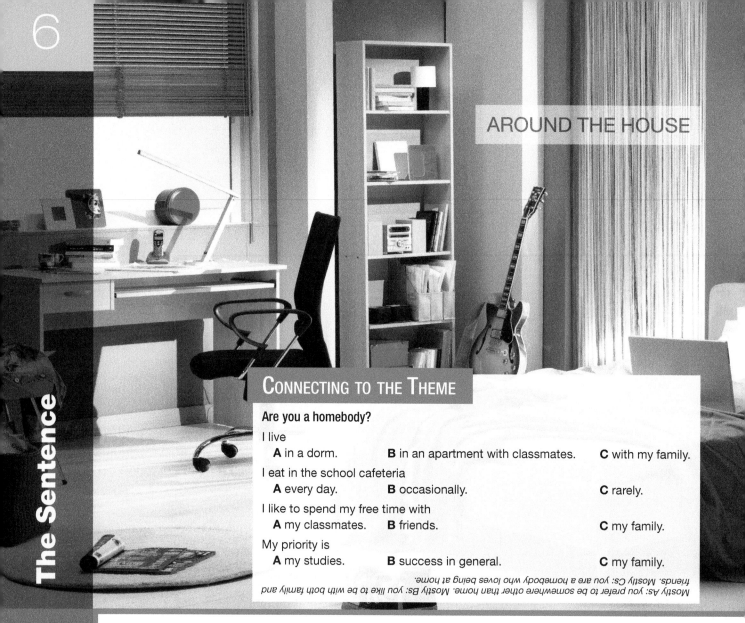

AROUND THE HOUSE

CONNECTING TO THE THEME

Are you a homebody?

I live
  A in a dorm.   **B** in an apartment with classmates.   **C** with my family.

I eat in the school cafeteria
  A every day.   **B** occasionally.   **C** rarely.

I like to spend my free time with
  A my classmates.   **B** friends.   **C** my family.

My priority is
  A my studies.   **B** success in general.   **C** my family.

Mostly As: you prefer to be somewhere other than home. Mostly Bs: you like to be with both family and friends. Mostly Cs: you are a homebody who loves being at home.

A. Skill Presentation

A **sentence** is a group of words that expresses a complete idea. In writing, a sentence begins with a capital letter. Sentences usually end with a period.

We need two bedrooms**.**

A sentence has two basic parts: a subject and a verb. The **subject** is the person or thing that does the action. The **verb** describes the action, or what the subject does. In statements, the subject comes before the verb.

We need two bedrooms.

My parents moved yesterday.

In this second example, the subject is *My parents*. They did the action. The verb is *moved*. *Moved* is the action that *my parents* did. This sentence expresses a complete idea. It also starts with a capital letter and ends with a period.

B. Over to You

1 **Read each sentence in the chart. Are the words in bold the subject or the verb? Check (✓) the box in the correct column.**

	SUBJECT	VERB
1. I **visited** my aunt yesterday.		
2. **She** moved last month.		
3. **Her new apartment** is in Springfield.		
4. It **is** near the train station.		
5. She **walks** to the supermarket.		
6. **The kitchen** has a new stove and refrigerator.		
7. The apartment **was** very messy.		
8. **My aunt** cleaned for three days.		
9. She **painted** the kitchen.		
10. Now **it** looks beautiful.		

2 **Read the sentences. Write the subject and verb.**

Subject	Verb	
_____	_____	**1** The Johnsons visited a new house yesterday.
_____	_____	**2** The house has three bedrooms.
_____	_____	**3** They looked at the kitchen first.
_____	_____	**4** The counters are old and broken.
_____	_____	**5** The refrigerator is broken, too.
_____	_____	**6** The front door opens very slowly.
_____	_____	**7** The Johnsons walked into every room.
_____	_____	**8** They talked about the house.

CHECK!

1 A sentence expresses a complete idea. Every sentence has a _____ and a verb.

2 The subject is a person or _____. The subject does the _____. The verb says what the subject does.

3 In statements, the subject comes _____ the verb.

C. Practice

1 Make sentences. Put the subject or verb in parentheses in the correct form. Don't forget to capitalize.

1 we in a nice apartment. (live)

_____

2 have a problem, though. (we)

_____

3 is always dirty. (the kitchen)

_____

4 looks very messy. (your room)

_____

5 I to the supermarket every week. (go)

_____

6 the food bad. (goes)

_____

7 I a clean apartment. (like)

_____

8 we some rules. (need)

_____

2 Match each paragraph (A–D) with the correct description (1–4).

___ **1** No mistakes   ___ **3** Mistakes with periods

___ **2** Mistakes with capital letters   ___ **4** Subject and verb in the wrong order

A   My family moved to a new apartment on 15th Street The building is on a beautiful block with lots of trees There is a supermarket nearby, so buying food is easy The train station is close. I can walk there in four minutes

B   my family moved to a new apartment on 15th Street. the building is on a beautiful block with lots of trees. there is a supermarket nearby, so buying food is easy. the train station is close. I can walk there in four minutes.

C   My family moved to a new apartment on 15th Street. The building is on a beautiful block with lots of trees. There is a supermarket nearby, so buying food is easy. The train station is close. I can walk there in four minutes.

D   My moved family to a new apartment on 15th Street. The building on a beautiful block is with lots of trees. There a supermarket is nearby, so buying food is easy. The is train station close. Can I walk there in four minutes.

D. Skill Quiz

Check (✓) the correct answer for each item.

1 ___ have a subject and a verb.
- ☐ a. Long sentences
- ☐ b. Some sentences
- ☐ c. All sentences

2 The subject of a sentence is
- ☐ a. the action that the person or thing does.
- ☐ b. the person or thing that does the action.
- ☐ c. a complete idea.

3 A verb is
- ☐ a. the action that a person or thing does.
- ☐ b. a person or thing that does the action.
- ☐ c. a complete idea.

4 In a statement,
- ☐ a. the subject comes first.
- ☐ b. the verb comes first.
- ☐ c. the period comes first.

5 *The apartment looks very messy.*
What is the subject in this sentence?
- ☐ a. very messy
- ☐ b. looks
- ☐ c. The apartment

6 *The building is not very nice.*
What is the subject in this sentence?
- ☐ a. not very nice
- ☐ b. The building
- ☐ c. is

7 *The closets are small.*
What is the verb in this sentence?
- ☐ a. The closets
- ☐ b. are
- ☐ c. small

8 *The kitchen a new oven.*
This sentence does not have
- ☐ a. a subject.
- ☐ b. a verb.
- ☐ c. a subject or a verb.

9 *At five o'clock.*
This sentence does not have
- ☐ a. a subject.
- ☐ b. a verb.
- ☐ c. a subject or a verb.

10 *Lives in Springfield.*
This sentence does not have
- ☐ a. a subject.
- ☐ b. a verb.
- ☐ c. a subject or a verb.

LOCAL ATTRACTIONS

CONNECTING TO THE THEME

What type of vacations do you enjoy?

When you visit somewhere for the first time, do you like to
    A visit museums and historical sites?   **B** shop, eat, and relax?

Who would you prefer to travel with?
    A Dr. Ramirez, a history professor   **B** John Anderson, a popular neighbor

Imagine you went to Sweden. Would you
    A learn some words in Swedish?   **B** only speak English?

Mostly As: you enjoy educational vacations. Mostly Bs: you enjoy relaxing vacations.

A. Skill Presentation

When you write, it is important to **capitalize** certain words. To capitalize a letter is to make it a capital. Proper nouns are always capitalized in English.

Follow three rules to make sure you capitalize proper nouns:

The **first rule** is to capitalize the first letter of people's names and titles.

    NAMES: Ana Garcia, Jorge Luis, Ursula Dietrich

Titles are introductions to a name such as *mister*, *missus*, *doctor*, and *professor*.

    TITLES: Mister John Howard, Missus Lara Sinclair
           Doctor Mariana Ariella, Professor Drake

The **second rule** is to capitalize the first letter of the names of countries, states, and provinces.

    Virginia, California, Ontario, Sweden

The **third rule** is to capitalize the first letter of the names of languages and nationalities. A person's nationality tells the country they are from.

For example, *Mexican* is the nationality of a person from Mexico. *Spanish* is a language someone from Mexico might speak.

    American, Arabic, Japanese, Italian

B. Over to You

1 **Read each sentence in the chart. Why is the word in bold in each sentence capitalized? Check (✓) the box in the correct column.**

	A PERSON'S TITLE	A COUNTRY OR A STATE	A LANGUAGE OR A NATIONALITY
1. The Romano family is **Italian**.			
2. **Ms.** Haley wants to take the tour with us.			
3. In **Georgia**, Centennial Olympic Park is a popular attraction.			
4. I speak **Spanish** very well.			
5. Greta is planning to drive to **Michigan**.			
6. There are historical attractions in **Virginia**.			
7. My history teacher is **Professor** Campbell.			
8. **Dr.** Cromwell is moving to Colorado.			
9. Lara Sinclair's best friend is **Russian**.			
10. The next country I want to visit is **Iceland**.			

2 **Read the paragraph. How many proper nouns do not have correct capitalization? Circle them and check (✓) the correct answer.**

My friend kyoung Mun is from South korea. She is going to move to San Diego, california next month. Her sister, Baye, is helping her move. They looked at a map and saw that San Diego is about 30 miles from mexico. They both want to learn more about San Diego. Baye asked her geography teacher, mr. Harris, about the city. He said many people there speak spanish, but there are also a lot of koreans. Baye and Kyoung are excited because they speak both korean and Spanish.

- [ ] a. There are four nouns with incorrect capitalization.
- [ ] b. There are six nouns with incorrect capitalization.
- [ ] c. There are eight nouns with incorrect capitalization.

CHECK!

1 When you write, remember to capitalize proper _____.

2 Capitalize the first letter of people's _____ and titles.

3 Capitalize the first letter of _____, states, and _____.

4 Capitalize the first letter of _____ and people's _____.

C. Practice

1 Check (✓) the answer that has correct capitalization

1 My name is ___, and I am your tour guide.
- ☐ a. Mr. Evans
- ☐ b. mr. evans
- ☐ c. mr. Evans

2 The information about the tour is available in ___.
- ☐ a. Spanish and Korean
- ☐ b. spanish and Korean
- ☐ c. Spanish and korean

3 I hope you enjoy your move from ___.
- ☐ a. Texas to Illinois
- ☐ b. texas to Illinois
- ☐ c. texas to illinois

4 They went to ___.
- ☐ a. Vietnam to learn vietnamese
- ☐ b. Vietnam to learn Vietnamese
- ☐ c. vietnam to learn Vietnamese

5 ___ visiting Pike's Peak.
- ☐ a. Professor Morris was in colorado
- ☐ b. professor Morris was in Colorado
- ☐ c. Professor Morris was in Colorado

6 In Belgium, people speak ___.
- ☐ a. French and Flemish
- ☐ b. french and Flemish
- ☐ c. French and flemish

7 I need to make an appointment with ___.
- ☐ a. Dr. Dewan
- ☐ b. dr. dewan
- ☐ c. dr. Dewan

8 My friend is ___.
- ☐ a. Brazilian but lives in the United States
- ☐ b. brazilian but lives in the united states
- ☐ c. brazilian but lives in the United States

2 Correct the sentences.

1 in santa fe, new mexico, there is a large plaza in the middle of the city.

_____

2 the first spanish settlers arrived there around 1608.

_____

3 many tourists visit santa fe every year, especially americans. they always want to see the old part of the city.

_____

4 my neighbors, professor and mrs. johnson, stopped by the visitor's center for information about the city.

_____

5 the city is historical because it is the oldest capital city in the united states.

_____

6 one of my favorite attractions there is the georgia O'keeffe Museum. it has thousands of visitors every year.

_____

D. Skill Quiz

Check (✓) the correct answer for each item.

1 A proper noun names
- a. a specific person, place, or thing.
- b. an important place or thing.
- c. a respected person.

2 Always capitalize
- a. adjectives and prepositions.
- b. languages and nationalities.
- c. important words.

3 Always capitalize
- a. names and titles.
- b. subjects and verbs.
- c. the last word in a sentence.

4 Choose the sentence with the correct capitalization.
- a. Mr. Santamaria learned to speak chinese.
- b. Mr. santamaria learned to speak Chinese.
- c. Mr. Santamaria learned to speak Chinese.

5 Choose the sentence with the correct capitalization.
- a. mrs. Abayas visited Spain, but she does not speak much spanish.
- b. Mrs. Abayas visited Spain, but she does not speak much spanish.
- c. Mrs. Abayas visited Spain, but she does not speak much Spanish.

6 Choose the sentence with the correct capitalization.
- a. My cousin martina owns a farm in Illinois.
- b. My cousin Martina owns a farm in Illinois.
- c. My cousin Martina owns a farm in illinois.

7 Choose the sentence with the correct capitalization.
- a. Josefina loves Croatia, Scotland, and Greece.
- b. Josefina loves Croatia, scotland, and greece.
- c. josefina loves Croatia, Scotland, and Greece.

8 Choose the sentence with the correct capitalization.
- a. Charlotte is going to visit south korea with her friend sela.
- b. Charlotte is going to visit South Korea with her friend sela.
- c. Charlotte is going to visit South Korea with her friend Sela.

9 Choose the sentence with the correct capitalization.
- a. Most Australians speak only English, but Martin also speaks German.
- b. Most australians speak only English, but Martin also speaks German.
- c. Most Australians speak only english, but Martin also speaks german.

10 Choose the sentence with the correct capitalization.
- a. Mr. Monroe is raising money to take students in his portuguese class to brazil.
- b. Mr. monroe is raising money to take students in his portuguese class to Brazil.
- c. Mr. Monroe is raising money to take students in his Portuguese class to Brazil.

Sentences with Objects

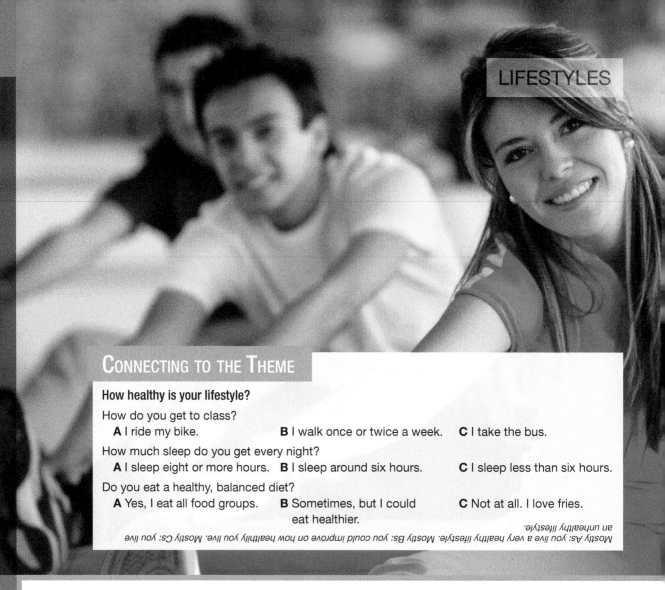

A. Skill Presentation

A sentence is a group of words and has two basic parts: a subject and a verb. The **subject** is the person or thing that does the action. The **verb** expresses the action that the subject does. Many sentences also have an object. The **object** is a noun. It answers the question *What?* or *Who?* about the verb.

> **Michael** often **takes** vacations.

Michael is the subject, *takes* is the verb, and *vacations* is the object. It answers the question about the verb *takes*: *What does Michael often take?* (Michael often takes vacations.)

> **Nancy** always **helps** her brother.

Who does Nancy help? *Her brother. Her brother* is the object in this sentence.

> **Her friends eat** healthy foods.

What do her friends eat? *Healthy foods. Healthy foods* is the object in this sentence.

In a statement, the order of words is subject, then verb, then object. In English, word order is important.

B. Over to You

1 Check (✓) the correct answer for each item.

1 *My friends changed their lifestyle.*
Choose the subject.

- ☐ a. My friends
- ☐ b. changed
- ☐ c. their lifestyle

2 *Jamie eats healthy foods.*
Choose the verb.

- ☐ a. Jamie
- ☐ b. eats
- ☐ c. healthy foods

3 *Tony drinks water at lunch.*
Choose the object.

- ☐ a. Tony
- ☐ b. drinks
- ☐ c. water

4 *They avoid stress at work.*
Choose the object.

- ☐ a. They
- ☐ b. avoid
- ☐ c. stress

5 *She rides her bike instead.*
Choose the verb.

- ☐ a. She
- ☐ b. rides
- ☐ c. her bike

6 *I live a better life.*
Choose the subject.

- ☐ a. I
- ☐ b. live
- ☐ c. a better life

2 Read each sentence in the chart. Are the words in bold the subject, the verb, or the object? Check (✓) the box in the correct column.

	SUBJECT	VERB	OBJECT
1. **My brother** is a newspaper editor.			
2. He **spends** all his time at work.			
3. He ignores **his diet**.			
4. He drinks **coffee** all day.			
5. He rarely **takes** a vacation.			
6. **He** checks his e-mail constantly.			
7. My brother loves **his job**.			
8. I **prefer** a relaxing lifestyle.			

CHECK!

1 Every sentence has a _____ and a verb. Many sentences also have an _____.

2 Objects are nouns. They answer the question _____? or _____? about the verb.

3 Word order is important in English. In a statement, the order is subject, then _____, then _____.

C. Practice

1   Make sentences. Put the subject, verb, or object in parentheses in the correct place. Don't forget to capitalize.

1   My cousins social people. (are)

_____

2   Your family is. (a social group)

_____

3   Every Sunday, she soccer with friends. (plays)

_____

4   My brother many groups of friends. (has)

_____

5   He often visits. (his fiancée)

_____

6   Eat dinner together every week. (they)

_____

7   Some people help. (others)

_____

8   My aunt helps in her neighborhood. (a friend)

_____

9   Has many benefits. (friendship)

_____

2   Read the paragraph and answer the questions. A sentence can be used more than once.

[1]My grandmother has a healthy lifestyle. [2]Every weekend, she visits her friends. [3]They take classes together. [4]For example, they study foreign languages. [5]They also teach classes. [6]Sometimes my grandmother teaches her friends. [7]She teaches a cooking class. [8]Sometimes her friends teach my grandmother. [9]One friend teaches line dancing. [10]My grandmother is very busy. [11]She has a lot of activities! [12]She also has a lot of friends.

1   In which sentences is *my grandmother* the subject?   ___, ___, and ___

2   In which sentence is *my grandmother* the object?   ___

3   In which sentence is *her friends* the subject?   ___

4   In which sentences is *her friends* the object?   ___ and ___

5   Which sentence does not have an object?   ___

D. Skill Quiz

Check (✓) the correct answer for each item.

1 ___ sentences have a subject and a verb.
- ☐ a. No
- ☐ b. Some
- ☐ c. All

2 ___ sentences have a subject, verb, and object.
- ☐ a. No
- ☐ b. Some
- ☐ c. All

3 The subject of a sentence is
- ☐ a. the action that the person or thing does.
- ☐ b. the person or thing that does the action.
- ☐ c. the noun that answers the question *Who?* or *What?* about the verb.

4 The object of a sentence is
- ☐ a. the action that the person or thing does.
- ☐ b. the person or thing that does the action.
- ☐ c. the noun that answers the question *Who?* or *What?*

5 The correct word order in English is
- ☐ a. subject, then verb, then object.
- ☐ b. verb, then subject, then object.
- ☐ c. object, then subject, then verb.

6 *I prefer a relaxing lifestyle.*
What is the subject in this sentence?
- ☐ a. I
- ☐ b. prefer
- ☐ c. lifestyle

7 *He rarely takes a vacation.*
What is the object in this sentence?
- ☐ a. rarely
- ☐ b. takes
- ☐ c. a vacation

8 *My friends ride their bicycles every day.*
What is the verb in this sentence?
- ☐ a. My friends
- ☐ b. ride
- ☐ c. their bicycles

9 *Our choices affect our health.*
What is the object in this sentence?
- ☐ a. Our choices
- ☐ b. affect
- ☐ c. our health

10 *We help our relatives.*
What is the subject in this sentence?
- ☐ a. We
- ☐ b. help
- ☐ c. our relatives

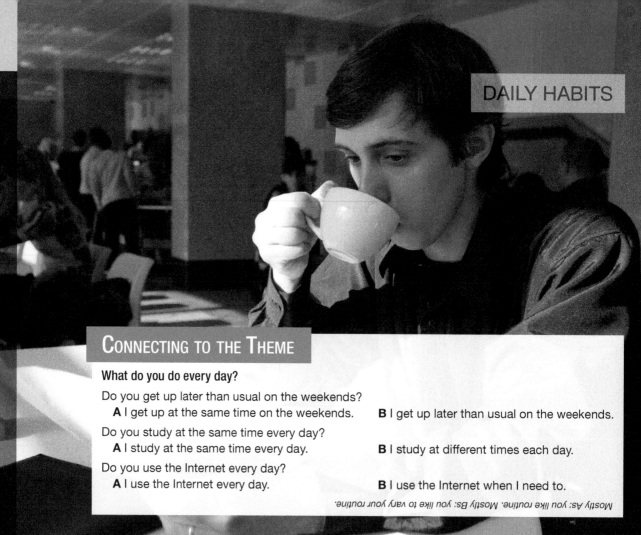

DAILY HABITS

CONNECTING TO THE THEME

What do you do every day?

Do you get up later than usual on the weekends?
   A I get up at the same time on the weekends.   **B** I get up later than usual on the weekends.

Do you study at the same time every day?
   A I study at the same time every day.   **B** I study at different times each day.

Do you use the Internet every day?
   A I use the Internet every day.   **B** I use the Internet when I need to.

Mostly As: you like routine. Mostly Bs: you like to vary your routine.

A. Skill Presentation

A sentence has a subject and a verb, and it expresses a complete idea.

    Students need more time.

The subject of this sentence is *Students*. The verb in this sentence is *need*. *Students need more time* expresses a complete idea.

A sentence that is missing a subject or a verb is called a **sentence fragment**.

    Need more time.

This is not a complete sentence. The subject (*Students*) is missing. When you write, remember to include a subject in every sentence.

    He very low grades.

This is also not a complete sentence. The verb is missing. Remember to include a verb in every sentence.

    He gets very low grades.

This is a complete sentence. *Gets* is the verb. *He* is the subject.

B. Over to You

1 Read each sentence in the chart. Decide if they are complete sentences or sentence fragments. Check (✓) the box in the correct column.

	COMPLETE SENTENCE	SENTENCE FRAGMENT
1. Many people need eight hours of sleep.		
2. Is important to get enough sleep.		
3. Some students study all night.		
4. That a bad habit.		
5. Often have memory problems.		
6. The brain works more slowly.		
7. Students poor grades.		
8. They make more mistakes.		
9. The students did well on the test.		
10. A regular schedule.		

2 Read each item. Decide if it needs a subject or a verb or if it is a complete sentence. Check (✓) the correct answer.

1 Likes to study all night.
- ☐ a. needs a subject
- ☐ b. needs a verb
- ☐ c. complete sentence

2 I good grades on my exams.
- ☐ a. needs a subject
- ☐ b. needs a verb
- ☐ c. complete sentence

3 Lisa keeps a regular schedule.
- ☐ a. needs a subject
- ☐ b. needs a verb
- ☐ c. complete sentence

4 Sleeps all day.
- ☐ a. needs a subject
- ☐ b. needs a verb
- ☐ c. complete sentence

5 I agree with the study.
- ☐ a. needs a subject
- ☐ b. needs a verb
- ☐ c. complete sentence

6 Has memory problems.
- ☐ a. needs a subject
- ☐ b. needs a verb
- ☐ c. complete sentence

CHECK!

1 Sentences need _____ and _____.

2 A sentence missing a subject or a verb is a _____.

C. Practice

1 **Read the paragraph. How many sentence fragments are there? Underline them and check (✓) the correct answer.**

Daniel is a college student. Has a bad habit. He likes to stay up all night. Sleeps all day. Daniel poor grades on his work. He has trouble concentrating. Wants to do his best. Daniel needs a better sleeping schedule. He an important exam tomorrow. He does not want to suffer from any memory problems. He plans to go to bed early tonight.

  ☐ a. There are two sentence fragments.
  ☐ b. There are five sentence fragments.
  ☐ c. There are seven sentence fragments.

2 **Read each sentence fragment in the chart. Decide if the subject or the verb is missing. Check (✓) the box in the correct column, then suggest a word to complete each sentence.**

	SUBJECT	VERB
1. They more mistakes.		
2. Wants to do her best.		
3. Some people more sleep than others.		
4. Sleeps all night.		
5. I medication when I have a headache.		
6. Bill always to bed at 10:00 p.m.		
7. Go to a concert or play together almost every week.		
8. A recent survey that many people don't get enough sleep.		
9. Who do not sleep enough get sick more easily.		
10. Who want to do well at college should keep a regular sleeping schedule.		

1 _____   6 _____

2 _____   7 _____

3 _____   8 _____

4 _____   9 _____

5 _____   10 _____

D. Skill Quiz

Check (✓) the correct answer for each item.

1 Every sentence needs
- ☐ a. a fragment.
- ☐ b. a subject and a verb.
- ☐ c. an adjective.

2 A sentence fragment is
- ☐ a. not a complete sentence.
- ☐ b. a complete sentence.
- ☐ c. a short answer.

3 Choose the sentence fragment.
- ☐ a. He studies all night.
- ☐ b. She gets poor grades.
- ☐ c. Is a bad habit.

4 Choose the sentence fragment.
- ☐ a. Daniel has an important exam.
- ☐ b. Daniel very low grades.
- ☐ c. Daniel does not go to sleep at night.

5 Choose the complete sentence.
- ☐ a. Agrees with the survey results.
- ☐ b. Have trouble thinking.
- ☐ c. The students took a sleep survey.

6 Choose the complete sentence.
- ☐ a. They stayed awake all night.
- ☐ b. Studied all day in the library.
- ☐ c. Their work not good.

7 *Students a regular schedule.*
- ☐ a. This sentence needs a verb.
- ☐ b. This sentence needs a subject.
- ☐ c. This sentence is complete.

8 *He takes medication for insomnia.*
- ☐ a. This sentence needs a verb.
- ☐ b. This sentence needs a subject.
- ☐ c. This sentence is complete.

9 *Suffers from poor concentration.*
- ☐ a. This sentence needs a verb.
- ☐ b. This sentence needs a subject.
- ☐ c. This sentence is complete.

10 *They more mistakes on their work.*
- ☐ a. This sentence needs a verb.
- ☐ b. This sentence needs a subject.
- ☐ c. This sentence is complete.

Prepositional Phrases

CULTURAL HOLIDAYS

Connecting to the Theme

How much do you know about holidays around the world?

Which national holiday takes place in January in Australia?

  A New Year's Day   **B** Australia Day   **C** both A and B

Which celebration is held around the world each year on March 8?

  A Labor Day   **B** Independence Day   **C** Women's Day

St. Patrick's Day is celebrated

  A in January.   **B** in May.   **C** in March.

Mostly As: you need to learn more about other cultures. Mostly Bs: you know some things, but could learn more. Mostly Cs: you know a lot about other cultures.

A. Skill Presentation

A **prepositional phrase** is a preposition followed by a **noun**. For example, look at these two prepositional phrases.

PREPOSITION	NOUN		PREPOSITION	NOUN
in	the United States		at	noon

Many prepositional phrases start with *in*, *on*, or *at*.

Use prepositional phrases to write about locations and time – *where* and *when* things happen.

  WHERE? in the United States, in Boston, on Market Street, at school

  WHEN? in 1865, in May, on Monday, on May 27, at 8:00 a.m.

Most prepositional phrases of time and location can go at the end of a sentence.

  There was a big event in Atlanta.

Some prepositional phrases can also go at the beginning of a sentence. When you write a prepositional phrase at the beginning of a sentence, remember to use a comma.

  In Atlanta, there was a big event.

When you write sentences with *be* as the main verb, do NOT put a prepositional phrase at the beginning of the sentence. The prepositional phrase must go after *be* when it is the main verb.

  On May 30, Memorial Day was. At the grave, we were. ✗

  Memorial Day was on May 30. We were at the grave. ✓

38

B. Over to You

1 **Read the paragraph. How many prepositional phrases are there? Underline them and check (✓) the correct answer.**

Arlington National Cemetery is in Arlington, Virginia. It has graves of soldiers. There are about 270,000 graves. Four million people visit the cemetery every year. Many people come on Memorial Day. They think it is important to remember soldiers who died. The cemetery usually closes at 7:00 p.m. In the winter, it closes earlier. Some people use maps, and some people take tours.

☐ a. There are five prepositional phrases.
☐ b. There are seven prepositional phrases.
☐ c. There are nine prepositional phrases.

2 **Read each sentence in the chart. Decide if the prepositional phrase in each sentence is in the correct place. Check (✓) the box in the correct column.**

	CORRECT	INCORRECT
1. Presidents' Day is a holiday in the United States.		
2. In the United States, many people do not work on Presidents' Day.		
3. The holiday is on a Monday.		
4. On a Monday, the holiday is.		
5. It is in February.		
6. In February, it is.		
7. We remember two important presidents on this day.		
8. On this day, we remember two important presidents.		
9. Two famous presidents' birthdays are in February.		
10. In February, two famous presidents' birthdays are.		

CHECK!

1 A prepositional phrase is a _____ followed by a _____, used to describe location and time. It can start with *in*, *on*, or *at*. If you write a prepositional phrase at the _____ of a sentence, remember to use a _____.

2 When you write sentences with *be* as the main verb, the prepositional phrase must go _____ *be*.

C. Practice

1 **Make sentences. Write the words in the correct order. Don't forget to add a period.**

1 ended | on November 11, 1918 | World War I

_____

2 died | a Canadian soldier | at 10:58 a.m.,

_____

3 in Le Havre, France | he | died

_____

4 the war | at 11:00 a.m. | ended

_____

5 celebrate | Remembrance Day | in Canada, | they

_____

6 started | Remembrance Day | in 1919

_____

7 there is | a moment of silence | at 10:58 a.m.,

_____

8 they | in other places | soldiers who died | remember

_____

2 **Rewrite the sentences that are incorrect. If the sentence is correct, write _CORRECT_.**

1 At my house the party was.

_____

2 On Monday, the holiday is.

_____

3 We at noon are meeting tomorrow.

_____

4 Adele in the United States lives.

_____

5 My friend lives on E 50th Street.

_____

6 At school, Stephen is today.

_____

7 In 1868, the first Memorial Day was.

_____

8 We finish school on June 26.

_____

D. Skill Quiz

Check (✓) the correct answer for each item.

1 What is a prepositional phrase?
- [ ] a. a sentence with several prepositions
- [ ] b. a preposition + a noun
- [ ] c. a group of prepositions

2 Which words are common prepositions?
- [ ] a. he, she, it
- [ ] b. where, when, why
- [ ] c. in, on, at

3 What information can prepositional phrases give?
- [ ] a. time or location
- [ ] b. who is doing the action
- [ ] c. why something happens

4 Which sentence is correct?
- [ ] a. Mexico celebrates its independence, on September 15.
- [ ] b. Mexico celebrates its independence on September 15.
- [ ] c. On September 15 Mexico celebrates, its independence.

5 Which sentence is correct?
- [ ] a. Mexico's biggest celebration is in Mexico City.
- [ ] b. In Mexico City, Mexico's biggest celebration is.
- [ ] c. Is in Mexico City, Mexico's biggest celebration.

6 Which sentence is correct?
- [ ] a. Canadians celebrate Thanksgiving, in October.
- [ ] b. In October Canadians, celebrate Thanksgiving.
- [ ] c. In October, Canadians celebrate Thanksgiving.

7 Which sentence is correct?
- [ ] a. American Thanksgiving is in November.
- [ ] b. Is in November, American Thanksgiving.
- [ ] c. In November, American Thanksgiving is.

8 Which sentence is correct?
- [ ] a. Some people celebrate New Year's Eve at friends' houses.
- [ ] b. At friends' houses some people celebrate, New Year's Eve.
- [ ] c. At friends' houses some people celebrate New Year's Eve.

9 Which sentence is correct?
- [ ] a. In November, the Day of the Dead is.
- [ ] b. The Day of the Dead is, in November.
- [ ] c. The Day of the Dead is in November.

10 Which sentence is correct?
- [ ] a. On the Day of the Dead, they make special bread.
- [ ] b. On the Day of the Dead they make special, bread.
- [ ] c. They make special bread, on the Day of the Dead.

Paragraph Formatting

CONNECTING TO THE THEME

Do you manage your time well? Read each sentence. Is it always, sometimes, or never true for you?

A always   **B** sometimes   **C** never

[1]I have many projects. [2]I have trouble prioritizing them or choosing the most important ones. [3]I start projects late, and then I don't finish them. [4]I don't like to work in groups because I delay the project for the other group members.

Mostly As: you are not managing your time well. Mostly Bs: your time could be managed more efficiently. Mostly Cs: your time management is excellent.

A. Skill Presentation

A paragraph is a group of sentences about one idea. A good paragraph is easy to read. It has correct formatting. This means that it looks a certain way and makes your writing easier to understand.

A paragraph is **indented**. To indent means to add space before the first sentence. Remember to only indent the first sentence in a paragraph.

    Time management is important. It helps you succeed. There are several helpful ways to manage your time. First, decide which tasks are most important. Second, make a to-do list of all the tasks. Third, put each task on your calendar. Finally, finish each task on time. With good time management, you will succeed.

A paragraph is a group of sentences, but it is NOT a list. Sentences in a paragraph continue on the same line, one after the other. Do not start each new sentence on a new line.

B. Over to You

1   Look at the paragraph. Read the questions and check (✓) the box in the correct column.

Time management is a good skill to learn. The first step is to write down every activity you do. My friends went to a movie last night. You should even write small things like drinking a cup of coffee. Then, write a number next to each activity. Activities with a 1 are very important. They should be done first. My brother writes lists in a small notebook. If you always follow your list, your time management skills will improve.

	YES	NO
1. Are all the sentences about one topic?		
2. Is the first sentence indented?		
3. Do the sentences come one after the other?		

2   Check (✓) the paragraph in each pair that has correct formatting.

1 ☐ **A**   Different people use different strategies for remembering tasks. My friends write reminders in notebooks. I use an electronic calendar. I use it for my homework and my job. My friend writes reminders on his hand. It is messy, but it works for him. It does not matter what strategy you use. It is only important that it works.

☐ **B** Different people use different strategies for remembering tasks. My friends write reminders in notebooks. I use an electronic calendar. I use it for my homework and my job. My friend writes reminders on his hand. It is messy, but it works for him. It does not matter what strategy you use. It is only important that it works.

2 ☐ **A**   Professor Marshall thinks deciding what is important is the best way to succeed in college. He asks his students to write down assignments. He tells them to think about how difficult each assignment is. He suggests starting with the most difficult assignment. Students should do easier assignments later. He thinks students who do this will succeed in school.

☐ **B**   Professor Marshall thinks deciding what is important is the best way to succeed in college. He asks his students to write down assignments. He tells them to think about how difficult each assignment is. He suggests starting with the most difficult assignment.
Students should do easier assignments later. He thinks students who do this will succeed in school.

CHECK!

1 A paragraph is a _____ of sentences about _____ idea.
2 A good paragraph is _____ to read. It has _____ formatting.
3 In a paragraph with correct formatting, the first sentence is _____.
The sentences in the paragraph come one after the other, on the same _____.

C. Practice

1 Circle the correct words.

1 The sentences in a paragraph are about *one idea | many ideas | bad ideas*.

2 A good paragraph is *difficult | easy | hard* to read because it has correct formatting.

3 Sentences in a paragraph *never | sometimes | always* start on a new line.

4 The first sentence in a paragraph is *indented | about a different topic | on a new line*.

5 Type about *two | five | fifteen* spaces to indent a paragraph.

6 A list of sentences is *a good paragraph | correct formatting | not a paragraph*.

2 Check (✓) the paragraph that has correct formatting.

☐ **A** Mr. Huang always prioritizes tasks to help him reach his goals at work.
For example, every morning he writes down the things he wants to do that day.
Then, he decides which tasks he must finish by the end of the day.
After that, he decides which tasks can wait.
He prioritizes well, so he knows he will always finish the most important things early.
He can do the tasks that are not very important the next day.
Mr. Huang gets a lot done at work because he does important tasks first.

☐ **B** Mr. Huang always prioritizes tasks to help him reach his goals at work. For example, every morning he writes down the things he wants to do that day. Then, he decides which tasks he must finish by the end of the day. After that, he decides which tasks can wait. He prioritizes well, so he knows he will always finish the most important things early. He can do the tasks that are not very important the next day. Mr. Huang gets a lot done at work because he does important tasks first.

☐ **C** Mr. Huang always prioritizes tasks to help him reach his goals at work. For example, every morning he writes down the things he wants to do that day.
Then, he decides which tasks he must finish by the end of the day. After that, he decides which tasks can wait.
He prioritizes well, so he knows he will always finish the most important things early. He can do the tasks that are not very important the next day.
Mr. Huang gets a lot done at work because he does important tasks first.

☐ **D** Mr. Huang always prioritizes tasks to help him reach his goals at work. For example, every morning he writes down the things he wants to do that day. Then, he decides which tasks he must finish by the end of the day. After that, he decides which tasks can wait. He prioritizes well, so he knows he will always finish the most important things early. He can do the tasks that are not very important the next day.
Mr. Huang gets a lot done at work because he does important tasks first.

D. Skill Quiz

Check (✓) the correct answer for each item.

1 What is a paragraph?
- a. a group of letters that make a word
- b. a group of words that make a sentence
- c. a group of sentences about one idea

2 To indent, add space
- a. before the second word.
- b. before the first sentence.
- c. before the last letter.

3 In a paragraph, indent
- a. only the first sentence.
- b. all the sentences.
- c. only the last sentence.

4 In a paragraph, each sentence begins
- a. in a separate list.
- b. on a new line.
- c. after the previous sentence.

5 In a paragraph, how can a writer make sure sentences are about the same idea?
- a. by giving some examples about each topic
- b. by including sentences about many different topics
- c. by removing sentences about different topics

6 In a paragraph, it is a mistake to include
- a. sentences about different ideas.
- b. sentences about one idea.
- c. sentences about good ideas.

7 Look at the paragraph below. Which sentence is about a different topic?
- a. There are only 24 hours in a day.
- b. Prioritizing can help.
- c. There is a list of classes in the main office.

8 Look at the paragraph below. Is the first sentence indented correctly?
- a. Yes. There are enough spaces.
- b. No. There are not enough spaces.
- c. No. There are too many spaces.

9 Look at the paragraph below. The writer used some correct formatting. What did the writer do correctly?
- a. All the sentences are in a list.
- b. All the sentences come one right after the other.
- c. All the sentences are on a new line.

10 Look at the paragraph below. Why is it easy to read?
- a. Because it is interesting.
- b. Because it has a title.
- c. Because it is formatted correctly.

Improving Time Management

There are only 24 hours in a day. Therefore, students need to manage their time well. Prioritizing can help. If students manage their time, they can do leisure activities, too. There are a few rules to follow. First, make a to-do list. There is a list of classes in the main office. Second, prioritize the to-do list by putting important things near the top. Third, start working. Do not waste time. Some waste can harm the environment. Use your time wisely, and you will succeed.

Topic Sentences

CONNECTING TO THE THEME

Which matches your idea of success?

A Having a lot of money proves I am successful. I am the owner of a successful financial company, and I work 60–70 hours a week. My work is the most important part of my life.

B Learning is the key to anything you want to do in life. I am a well-known professor at a local college, and I help young people from poor areas achieve academic success.

C Money cannot make you happy. I don't mind what work I do – I work just enough to feed my family but not more. Spending time with my family is the most important thing to me.

A: money is success. B: knowledge is success. C: happiness is success.

A. Skill Presentation

A paragraph is a group of sentences about one topic. The **topic sentence** tells us the main idea of the paragraph. The topic sentence often comes at the beginning of a paragraph.

Look at these examples:

TSChris Gardner is famous for his life story. He used to be poor and homeless. Now he is a successful businessman, writer, and speaker.

TSMany people face challenges in life. Some people have a hard time finding a job. Other people do not always have much money.

TSThe music executive heard the band play. He helped them become very famous.

TSThe music store manager lost his job. His store was not making enough money.

B. Over to You

1 **Match each paragraph (1–4) with the best topic sentence (a–d).**

a Chris had a young son.

b Chris likes to speak about his hard times and how he didn't give up.

c It was not easy being homeless.

d Chris wrote a book about his experiences.

1 ___ There was not enough money. Chris had to find different places to sleep at night. Sometimes he and his son slept in a train station. Chris had to find free food to eat. He often felt discouraged.

2 ___ His name is Chris, too. He was very young when he and his father were homeless. He does not remember much about the experience. His strongest memory is that he and his father moved around a lot.

3 ___ It is the story of how he lived when he was homeless. The book shows that Chris never gave up. It describes how he became very successful.

4 ___ He has a talent for public speaking. Groups often invite him to talk about his life. They want to learn from his life story. Chris wants people to know that they can be successful, too.

2 **The sentences from these paragraphs are in the wrong order. Find and check (✓) the topic sentences.**

1 ☐ a. Chris did not know his father.
☐ b. He lived with his mother and stepfather.
☐ c. His mother spent time in prison.
☐ d. Chris Gardner did not have an easy childhood.
☐ e. The family was poor.

2 ☐ a. The book was on the best-seller list for more than four months.
☐ b. It was translated into 14 languages.
☐ c. In 2006, Chris Gardner wrote a very popular book about his life.
☐ d. The book was later made into a movie.

3 ☐ a. He is a famous American actor and musician.
☐ b. His young son, Jaden Smith, was also in the movie.
☐ c. Will enjoyed playing the part of Gardner.
☐ d. Will Smith played the part of Chris Gardner in a movie about Gardner's life.

CHECK!

1 Every paragraph needs a _____ sentence.

2 The topic sentence tells us the _____ idea of the paragraph. It is often the _____ sentence in a paragraph.

C. Practice

1 Check (✓) the best topic sentence for each paragraph.

1 ___ Often their jobs are low-paying. There is not enough money for housing. They may have to decide between having a place to live or having food to eat. Some people think that homeless people do not want to work. This is not true.

☐ a. Most homeless people only work when they have to.
☐ b. Many homeless people have jobs, but they cannot afford a place to live.
☐ c. Having a house is more important than food.

2 ___ Lopez is a writer for a Los Angeles newspaper. One day, he heard Ayers playing music on the street. Ayers had a lot of talent. However, he was homeless and had some problems. The movie tells how Lopez helped Ayers find help.

☐ a. The Soloist is a movie about a newspaper writer, Steve Lopez, and a homeless musician, Nathaniel Ayers.
☐ b. Nathaniel Ayers was born in 1951.
☐ c. Steve Lopez went to San Jose State University.

3 ___ They have more than 200 food banks. They provide food for people in all 50 states. Feeding America gives food to more than 37 million people each year. Many of these are children and elderly people. Feeding America is an important charity.

☐ a. There are many hungry people in South America.
☐ b. Feeding America helps people all over the world find places to live.
☐ c. Feeding America gives food to hungry people in the United States.

2 Match each topic sentence (1–5) with two correct supporting sentences (a–j).

1 Chris Gardner has many talents.   ___ ___

2 Professor Kate Ortiz is very successful.   ___ ___

3 The fashion magazine described some new styles.   ___ ___

4 My brother is an actor.   ___ ___

5 Alexander Graham Bell was an important inventor.   ___ ___

a The color yellow is not fashionable this year.

b He got the part.

c He is a successful businessman.

d He also experimented with hearing devices.

e She has won awards for her medical research.

f He is most famous for inventing the telephone.

g He is an excellent public speaker, too.

h None of the top designers are using heavy fabrics.

i Yesterday, he went to an audition for a new movie.

j She also teaches a popular biology course.

D. Skill Quiz

Check (✓) the correct answer for each item.

1 A paragraph is a group of sentences about
- [ ] a. many topics.
- [ ] b. one topic.
- [ ] c. two topics.

2 The topic sentence tells the ___ of a paragraph.
- [ ] a. main idea
- [ ] b. conclusion
- [ ] c. title

3 The topic sentence often comes
- [ ] a. at the end of a paragraph.
- [ ] b. in the middle of a paragraph.
- [ ] c. at the beginning of a paragraph.

4 Choose the best topic sentence for a paragraph about people in San Francisco.
- [ ] a. There are several reasons why many people live in San Francisco.
- [ ] b. San Francisco is a wonderful place.
- [ ] c. Some of the best restaurants in the United States are in San Francisco.

5 Choose the best topic sentence for a paragraph about starting a new business.
- [ ] a. Many people say you should never give up.
- [ ] b. It is important to have a plan before you create a new business.
- [ ] c. Money is necessary, and you should learn how to use it.

6 Choose the best topic sentence for a paragraph about the talents of Chris Gardner.
- [ ] a. Chris Gardner used to be homeless, but now he is successful.
- [ ] b. Chris Gardner wrote a popular book.
- [ ] c. Chris Gardner is an excellent businessman, writer, and public speaker.

7 Choose the best topic sentence for a paragraph about graduating from college.
- [ ] a. Students who had good grades often have better jobs now.
- [ ] b. Students at my college can choose from more than 20 majors.
- [ ] c. Students usually feel successful when they get a college degree.

8 Choose the best topic sentence for a paragraph about Jaden Smith.
- [ ] a. Jaden Smith has a younger sister named Willow.
- [ ] b. Jaden Smith's first movie role was in a film about Chris Gardner's life.
- [ ] c. Jaden Smith has starred in several popular movies.

9 Choose the best topic sentence for a paragraph about Nathaniel Ayers.
- [ ] a. Nathaniel Ayers was a talented musician who became homeless.
- [ ] b. Nathaniel Ayers met a reporter.
- [ ] c. There are many things to do in Los Angeles.

10 Read the best topic sentence for this paragraph:
___ *Mrs. Zheng grew up in Guangzhou, China. She always wanted to live in the United States. When she was 20, she learned to cook. Then, when she was 25, she moved to Maryland. She opened a small Chinese restaurant. Now her restaurant is very popular. Ying Zheng's business is a success.*
- [ ] a. Ying Zheng moved to the United States to open her own restaurant.
- [ ] b. Ying Zheng traveled to Italy last year to learn how to cook Italian food.
- [ ] c. Ying Zheng had kind and caring parents.

BUSINESS IDEAS

Supporting Sentences

A. Skill Presentation

A paragraph is a group of sentences about one topic. The **topic sentence** tells the main idea of the paragraph. It usually comes first. **Supporting sentences** give more information about the topic sentence. They usually follow it. They are directly related to the main idea.

> [TS]Viola Vaughn is a social entrepreneur[1]. [SS]She started a school for girls in Africa.

The paragraph is about Viola Vaughn as a businesswoman. The supporting sentence is directly related to the main idea. It gives more information about one of Viola Vaughn's businesses – she started a school for girls in Africa. The other sentences in this paragraph will also relate to Viola's businesses. They will give more information about them.

---

[1]**entrepreneur:** someone who starts their own business, especially when it involves seeing a new opportunity

B. Over to You

1 Match each topic sentence (1–5) with the correct supporting sentence (a–e).

___ 1 Viola Vaughn is a social entrepreneur.

___ 2 The schools distribute free school supplies.

___ 3 Each school has an after-school program.

___ 4 Viola's business grew quickly.

___ 5 Dr. Vaughn has a traveling library that goes to small towns once a month.

a They give away notebooks, paper, and pens.

b There are over 2,500 girls now.

c She gives education to girls living in poverty.

d Every afternoon, teachers tutor the girls.

e Local children can check out books for free.

2 Read the topic sentence and the first supporting sentence. Then read each sentence in the chart, and decide if it is related to the main idea or not. Check (✓) the box in the correct column.

Topic Sentence: Jack Weil started a Western-style clothing business in 1946.

First Supporting Sentence: He became one of the oldest businessmen in the United States.

	RELATED	NOT RELATED
1. Weil named the company Rockmount Ranch Wear.		
2. People in big cities do not wear Western-style clothing.		
3. The store's most popular product was a cowboy-style shirt with snaps.		
4. Weil's granddaughter had a dog named Rocky.		
5. Rockmount Ranch Wear distributed the shirts all over the world.		
6. Many cowboys live in Colorado.		
7. Weil worked at the store every day until he was 107 years old.		
8. People over 80 should not work.		

CHECK!

1 A _____ is a group of sentences about one topic.

2 _____ sentences in a paragraph give more _____ about the topic sentence. They are directly related to the main _____.

C. Practice

1 **Read each topic sentence. Check (✓) the best supporting sentence.**

1 Jack Weil named his company Rockmount Ranch Wear.

☐ a. He chose the name because he loved the Rocky Mountains.
☐ b. He lived in Colorado.

2 Weil was one of the oldest businessmen in America.

☐ a. Famous actors wore his shirts.
☐ b. He worked until he was 107 years old.

3 Jack Weil enjoyed talking to customers.

☐ a. For example, he liked to talk about his granddaughter's dog, Rocky.
☐ b. People bought many shirts.

4 Rockmount Ranch Wear sold Western-style clothing.

☐ a. The most popular product was the cowboy-style shirt with snaps.
☐ b. Not many businessmen wear Western-style shirts.

5 Fred DeLuca had a new concept when he opened the first Subway restaurant.

☐ a. He was born in 1948.
☐ b. He wanted to use very fresh foods.

6 The Subway restaurant company is very successful.

☐ a. There are over 33,000 locations in 92 countries.
☐ b. They make bread every day.

2 **Match each topic sentence (1–5) with two correct supporting sentences (a–j).**

1 My friend has a great business idea. ___ ___

2 Students donate used books at our college bookstore. ___ ___

3 Many children living in poverty don't get new clothes very often. ___ ___

4 My group is working on a report about children in Africa. ___ ___

5 After two years, the store had no more money. ___ ___

a They sometimes don't have food, too.

b The store gives the books to students in need.

c They did not make a profit.

d She wants to sell coffee in our local park.

e We will also make suggestions about how we can help them.

f Their families have very little money.

g So they had to shut down.

h Maybe she'll even sell cakes and cookies, too.

i They also supply pens and pencils.

j We are going to write about all the facts we find.

D. Skill Quiz

Check (✓) the correct answer for each item.

1 A paragraph is a group of sentences
- ☐ a. about several topics.
- ☐ b. about supporting sentences.
- ☐ c. about one topic.

2 A topic sentence
- ☐ a. is one kind of supporting sentence.
- ☐ b. tells the main idea of a paragraph.
- ☐ c. tells you the paragraph is over.

3 Supporting sentences in a paragraph
- ☐ a. are directly related to the main idea.
- ☐ b. do not give information about the main idea.
- ☐ c. are about different topics.

4 Supporting sentences can
- ☐ a. give more information about the main idea.
- ☐ b. start a new paragraph.
- ☐ c. repeat the topic sentence.

5 Choose the best supporting sentence for this topic sentence: *The businessman is a social entrepreneur.*
- ☐ a. He is a happy and friendly person.
- ☐ b. He wants to help people in need.
- ☐ c. He likes to go to parties with friends.

6 Choose the best supporting sentence for this topic sentence: *Many of the girls live in poverty.*
- ☐ a. They live in towns with their families.
- ☐ b. They bake bread and make dolls to sell.
- ☐ c. They do not have enough money.

7 Choose the best supporting sentence for this topic sentence: *A traveling library goes to small towns once a month.*
- ☐ a. The local children can get books to read.
- ☐ b. The people in the towns cannot read.
- ☐ c. Books are not important in small towns.

8 Choose the best supporting sentence for this topic sentence: *A group of girls in the United States donated money to girls in Africa.*
- ☐ a. They learned about Asia and Europe, too.
- ☐ b. They wanted to help the girls in need.
- ☐ c. They had to write a report about African schools.

9 Choose the best supporting sentence for this topic sentence: *Viola Vaughn taught the girls about business.*
- ☐ a. She taught them how to sell products.
- ☐ b. She gave them free school supplies.
- ☐ c. She expanded her schools to five locations.

10 Choose the best supporting sentence for this topic sentence: *Jack Weil was one of the oldest businessmen in the United States.*
- ☐ a. He lived in Colorado.
- ☐ b. He was a social entrepreneur.
- ☐ c. He worked when he was 107 years old.

Concluding Sentences

CONNECTING TO THE THEME

Which would you like your life story to be like?

A Daniel moved from Greece to the United States and became a successful businessman. He sells yogurt and olive oil from his village in Greece. These healthy and delicious foods became very popular with the American people. He left Greece and found financial success with a business in the United States.

B Emily studied hard at school and achieved academic success. She is now a doctor and researcher. She works hard and hopes to find a cure for cancer. She wants her research to help all of humanity. Her commitment helped her find great success.

C Mr. Hislop helps all students in his community get the best education they can. He teaches students at the local high school. He also teaches students at home who cannot get to school because they are disabled. At night, he teaches classes for students who have jobs during the day. He works hard to help everyone get a good education.

A: you are interested in financial success. B: you would like to give a gift to humanity. C: you would like to help your community.

A. Skill Presentation

All paragraphs have a **topic sentence**. The topic sentence tells the main idea of the paragraph. All paragraphs end with a concluding sentence. The concluding sentence is usually the last sentence in a paragraph. A concluding sentence can repeat the main idea of the paragraph using different words.

Look at this topic sentence from a paragraph about Julia Child.

TSJulia Child was well known for French cooking.

Now look at the concluding sentence from the same paragraph.

CSJulia Child was famous for making French food.

B. Over to You

1 Match each topic sentence (1–5) with the correct concluding sentence (a–e).

1 Julia Child had a good time going places with her mother and father. ___

2 Julia Child had a TV show called Baking with Julia. ___

3 Julia Child wrote a cookbook about dinner parties. ___

4 Julia Child and her husband were happily married for almost 50 years. ___

5 Julia Child's kitchen is on display at a museum in Washington, D.C. ___

a Today, visitors can see where the French chef cooked and worked.

b The Childs had a long and happy marriage.

c She gave a lot of baking ideas on this TV program.

d Her book had many ideas about meals to make for friends.

e Julia enjoyed traveling with her parents.

2 Read each paragraph. Check (✓) the correct concluding sentence.

1   Steve Jobs was always interested in technology. He studied technology in high school. After class, he often visited the Hewlett-Packard company. People at the company gave speeches about technology. These speeches inspired him. Many years later, the company gave him a job. Jobs learned a lot about computers at Hewlett-Packard. He eventually helped start a famous computer company. ___

☐   a. He met his future business partner at Hewlett-Packard.
☐   b. Technology was always a big part of Jobs's life.
☐   c. He got married in 1991 and had four children.

2   Peter Buffett had loving parents and a normal childhood. He was not spoiled by his wealthy father. Peter's father is Warren Buffett, one of the richest people in the world. Peter lived with his family in Omaha, Nebraska. They did not have a big house or expensive things. His parents taught him to respect other people and to do work that he loved. ___

☐   a. When he was young, Peter Buffet's life was similar to many other children's.
☐   b. When he got older, Peter became a musician and an author.
☐   c. Peter's father still lives in the family house in Omaha.

CHECK!

1 The concluding sentence is usually the _____ sentence in a paragraph.

2 The concluding sentence can _____ the main idea of the paragraph using _____ words.

C. Practice

1 The sentences from these paragraphs are in the wrong order. Read each topic sentence, then find and check (✓) the correct concluding sentence.

1 As a child, my cousin spent six hours on the computer every day.

- ☐ a. He was always watching movies online and sending e-mails.
- ☐ b. He did not get enough exercise.
- ☐ c. My cousin spent too much time at the computer when he was young.
- ☐ d. He even ate at the computer.

2 Ms. Lopez's daughter enjoyed learning with computers.

- ☐ a. She often played math games online.
- ☐ b. She thought online learning was fun.
- ☐ c. She did many reading and spelling activities, too.
- ☐ d. She did online activities to learn history, science, and even business.

3 Bill Gates does not allow his daughter to spend much time on the computer.

- ☐ a. Gates thinks it is important to limit his children's computer time.
- ☐ b. When she was 10, she could spend 45 minutes a day playing on the computer.
- ☐ c. Gates only let her visit certain websites.
- ☐ d. She was also allowed to use the computer to do homework.

2 Choose the correct concluding sentence for each topic sentence. Write *a* or *b*.

1 Julia Child's first TV show was very popular. ___

a. Julia Child was on several shows.
b. Many people enjoyed Julia Child's first show.

2 Children should be active. ___

a. Young people need to play and run.
b. Even teens need exercise.

3 Our community benefits from having two schools. ___

a. One is for older students, and one is for younger students.
b. The advantage to the community is having more than one school.

4 Our company sells office supplies. ___

a. They can provide for all your office needs.
b. It is a big business with many stores.

5 Some wealthy people do not have to work. ___

a. Rich people have enough money to live without working.
b. The solution would be to have a lot of money and not go to work.

6 The students do volunteer work on weekends. ___

a. Many students help clean up the trash from beaches.
b. They enjoy helping others in their free time.

D. Skill Quiz

Check (✓) the correct answer for each item.

1 A good paragraph has one topic sentence, supporting sentences, and

   ☐ a. several main ideas.
   ☐ b. extra information.
   ☐ c. one concluding sentence.

2 A concluding sentence is usually

   ☐ a. the first sentence in a paragraph.
   ☐ b. the second sentence in a paragraph.
   ☐ c. the last sentence in a paragraph.

3 The concluding sentence often repeats

   ☐ a. the supporting sentences in the paragraph.
   ☐ b. all the sentences in the paragraph.
   ☐ c. the main idea in the paragraph.

4 A concluding sentence can use

   ☐ a. the same words as the topic sentence.
   ☐ b. different words from the topic sentence.
   ☐ c. words about a new main idea.

5 Choose the concluding sentence that goes with this topic sentence: *Steve Jobs is best known for starting a computer company.*

   ☐ a. Today, many families have computers at home.
   ☐ b. Today, Jobs is famous for starting this company.
   ☐ c. Today, computers cost less than they did ten years ago.

6 Choose the concluding sentence that goes with this topic sentence: *Peter Buffett had a very happy childhood.*

   ☐ a. Buffett enjoyed his time as a child.
   ☐ b. Warren Buffett is very rich and is Peter's father.
   ☐ c. Peter Buffett grew up to be a musician.

7 Choose the concluding sentence that goes with this topic sentence: *Julia Child enjoyed traveling as a child and as an adult.*

   ☐ a. She ate at many French restaurants.
   ☐ b. Julia eventually started a cooking school in France.
   ☐ c. Julia had a lifelong interest in travel.

8 Choose the concluding sentence that goes with this topic sentence: *Julia and Paul Child had a long and successful marriage.*

   ☐ a. Paul Child was ten years older than Julia.
   ☐ b. They were happily married for almost 50 years.
   ☐ c. Julia learned to cook because of Paul.

9 Choose the concluding sentence that goes with this topic sentence: *Too much time at the computer is bad for children's health.*

   ☐ a. Children who spend a lot of time at the computer may become unhealthy.
   ☐ b. Parents should volunteer at the school computer lab.
   ☐ c. Some children can learn to read on the computer.

10 Choose the concluding sentence that goes with this topic sentence: *Some computer games can make learning fun for children.*

   ☐ a. Teachers worry about children who cannot read.
   ☐ b. Too many computers in one house can be a problem.
   ☐ c. Many children enjoy computer activities with spelling and math games.

Simple and Compound Sentences

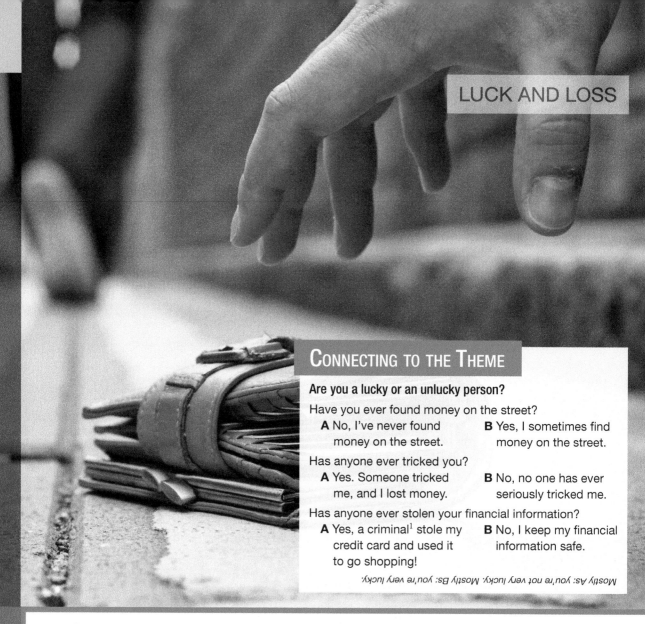

CONNECTING TO THE THEME

Are you a lucky or an unlucky person?

Have you ever found money on the street?

A No, I've never found money on the street.

B Yes, I sometimes find money on the street.

Has anyone ever tricked you?

A Yes. Someone tricked me, and I lost money.

B No, no one has ever seriously tricked me.

Has anyone ever stolen your financial information?

A Yes, a criminal[1] stole my credit card and used it to go shopping!

B No, I keep my financial information safe.

Mostly As: you're not very lucky. Mostly Bs: you're very lucky.

A. Skill Presentation

A **simple sentence** has one subject–verb group, and it expresses one complete idea.

> **Martin answered** a text message.

A **compound sentence** has at least two subject–verb groups. It expresses at least two complete ideas.

> **Martin sent** a text message, and **Ronaldo read** it.

In a compound sentence, the two complete ideas are joined by a **conjunction**. Some conjunctions are *and*, *but*, and *so*. When you write, put a comma before the conjunction.

> Alex gave them his credit card number, **and** they used it.

> She wanted my credit card number, **but** I said no.

> My mother and father thought they were being cheated, **so** they said no.

....

[1]**criminal:** someone who breaks the law

B. Over to You

1 **Read each sentence in the chart. Decide if it is a simple sentence or a compound sentence. Check (✓) the box in the correct column.**

	SIMPLE SENTENCE	COMPOUND SENTENCE
1. Sheila received a text message from a stranger.		
2. Marsha received a text message from a stranger, but she did not reply.		
3. A stranger tricked Miguel over e-mail last year.		
4. Don received a phone call from a stranger, so he hung up.		
5. Antonio always uses a credit card, but Patricia pays with cash.		
6. Charlotte sends text messages to her friends.		

2 **Check (✓) the correct answer for each item.**

1 Choose the compound sentence.

- [ ] a. Charles bought a new cell phone.
- [ ] b. Charles bought a new phone, but Carmela kept the same phone.
- [ ] c. Charles wants to buy a new cell phone tomorrow.

2 Choose the simple sentence.

- [ ] a. Esther got a text message from a strange number.
- [ ] b. Esther got a text message, and she deleted it.
- [ ] c. Esther got a text message, but she did not reply to it.

3 Choose the simple sentence.

- [ ] a. Kyoung sent Ms. Rankin an e-mail, and she replied.
- [ ] b. Kyoung sent Ms. Rankin an e-mail, but she did not reply.
- [ ] c. Kyoung sent Ms. Rankin an e-mail this morning.

4 Choose the compound sentence.

- [ ] a. Chen was tricked by the text message, but Tsai was not tricked.
- [ ] b. Chen was tricked by a text message.
- [ ] c. Tsai is not usually tricked.

CHECK!

1 A simple sentence has one _____ group. It expresses _____ complete idea.

2 A compound sentence has at least _____ subject–verb groups. It expresses at least _____ complete ideas.

3 A compound sentence has a _____ such as *and*, *but*, or *so*.

C. Practice

1 Read each pair of sentences in the chart. Decide if the sentences are simple sentences or compound sentences. Check (✓) the box in the correct column.

	SIMPLE SENTENCE	COMPOUND SENTENCE
1. a. Maria got a text message from Amy.		
b. Maria got a text message, and she replied to it.		
2. a. A stranger called Amelia, and she hung up.		
b. Amelia hung up the phone.		
3. a. Pablo sent an e-mail yesterday.		
b. Pablo sent an e-mail, but he did not call.		
4. a. Michael lost his phone, and someone used it.		
b. Someone used Michael's phone.		
5. a. Amanda prefers checks.		
b. Amanda prefers checks, but Ricardo uses cash.		

2 Read each paragraph and answer the questions.

1 ¹Criminals often lie to get what they want. ²They often use text messages to tell these lies. ³A criminal sends a text message to someone. ⁴The text message tells the person to call their bank. ⁵There is a telephone number in the text message, so the person calls the number. ⁶They give their credit card number. ⁷Then the criminal uses the person's credit card number and buys things. ⁸This trick can happen to anyone, so if you get a text message like this, do not reply.

1 How many simple sentences does the text have? ___ Sentences: _____

2 How many compound sentences does the text have? ___ Sentences: _____

3 What conjunctions are used? _____

4 Are commas used before the conjunctions? _____

2 ¹Criminals often lie to get what they want, and they often use text messages to tell these lies. ²A criminal sends a text message to someone. ³The text message tells the person to call their bank. ⁴There is a telephone number in the text message, so the person calls the number. ⁵They give their credit card number, but then the criminal uses the person's credit card number and buys things. ⁶This trick can happen to anyone. ⁷If you get a text message like this, do not reply.

1 How many simple sentences does the text have? ___ Sentences: _____

2 How many compound sentences does the text have? ___ Sentences: _____

3 What conjunctions are used? _____

4 Are commas used before the conjunctions? _____

D. Skill Quiz

Check (✓) the correct answer for each item.

1 A simple sentence
- ☐ a. has two subject–verb groups.
- ☐ b. always has a conjunction.
- ☐ c. expresses one complete idea.

2 A compound sentence
- ☐ a. has two subject–verb groups.
- ☐ b. has only one verb.
- ☐ c. has exactly one complete idea.

3 An example of a conjunction is
- ☐ a. *and.*
- ☐ b. *from.*
- ☐ c. *together.*

4 A compound sentence always has
- ☐ a. a question mark.
- ☐ b. a comma.
- ☐ c. an apostrophe.

5 Choose the simple sentence.
- ☐ a. Carmen lost her phone, so she bought a new one.
- ☐ b. Carmen lost her phone yesterday afternoon at the mall.
- ☐ c. Carmen lost her phone, but she did not buy a new one.

6 Choose the simple sentence.
- ☐ a. Anna pays her bills on time, but Pablo pays his late.
- ☐ b. Anna always pays her credit card bill on time.
- ☐ c. Anna pays her bills on time, so she does not have late fees.

7 Choose the compound sentence.
- ☐ a. A criminal stole Wei's credit card number.
- ☐ b. Wei lost her credit card, so she canceled it.
- ☐ c. Wei never uses her credit card.

8 Choose the compound sentence.
- ☐ a. A stranger called Katia, and she hung up.
- ☐ b. A stranger called Katia on the phone.
- ☐ c. Katia did not answer the phone.

9 Choose the compound sentence.
- ☐ a. Mercedes does not charge anything to her credit card.
- ☐ b. Mercedes likes to pay for things with cash.
- ☐ c. Mercedes pays with cash, so she rarely uses a credit card.

10 Choose the compound sentence.
- ☐ a. Someone tricked David over text message.
- ☐ b. David replied to the text message from a stranger.
- ☐ c. A stranger sent a text to David, and he replied to it.

Simple Sentences with Two Verbs

EATING HABITS

CONNECTING TO THE THEME

How much do you know about foods that can help you learn?

Blueberries keep your brain active and help you	**A** learn.	**B** read.
Avocados help your brain get more	**A** oxygen.	**B** rest.
Eggs improve your memory and help you	**A** concentrate.	**B** sleep.
Salmon is rich in Omega-3 fatty acids that protect your	**A** brain.	**B** eyes.

Mostly As: you know a lot about what foods help you learn. Mostly Bs: you need to learn more about what foods will help you learn.

A. Skill Presentation

A simple sentence has a subject and a verb, and it expresses a complete idea. The subject is the person or thing that does the action. The verb expresses the action.

SUBJECT VERB
Food helps you.

Some simple sentences have two verbs. The verbs express two actions by the same subject.

SUBJECT VERB   VERB
Food helps you and **hurts** you.

Help and *hurt* are two things that food does.

In a simple sentence, you can join two verbs with a **conjunction**. Some common conjunctions are *and* and *or*.

Sheri shops **and** cooks on Saturday.

John buys fast food **or** cooks at home.

If both verbs are negative, use the words *do not* only once. Use the conjunction *or*.

We do not buy **or** eat unhealthy food.

B. Over to You

1 Read each sentence in the chart. Decide if it has one or two verbs. Check (✓) the box in the correct column.

	ONE VERB	TWO VERBS
1. Carrots keep eyes healthy.		
2. Blueberries are good for the skin.		
3. Healthy oils help the skin.		
4. Water cleans the skin.		
5. Some food is bad for the skin.		
6. Most people need about eight hours of sleep.		
7. Julia does not sleep or eat well.		
8. She drinks coffee and eats dinner late at night.		
9. Steven sleeps well at night.		
10. He does not drink or eat anything after 7:00 p.m.		

2 Read the paragraph. How many verbs are there? Circle them and check (✓) the correct answer.

   Some drinks benefit your body. Milk builds strong bones and helps your teeth. Green tea prevents some diseases and helps your heart. Water is very good for your body. It cleans the skin. Some drinks are bad for you. Cola does not help your body or benefit your skin.

☐ a. There are seven verbs.
☐ b. There are nine verbs.
☐ c. There are ten verbs.

CHECK!

1 A simple sentence can have _____ verbs. The verbs express two actions by the same subject.

2 You can join the _____ with *and* or *or*.

3 When the two verbs are _____, write *do not*, *does not*, or *did not* only _____. Use the conjunction _____.

C. Practice

1 Make sentences. Write the words in the correct order. Don't forget to add a period.

1 eats | Linda | healthy food | and drinks

_____

2 or play sports | do not exercise | I

_____

3 to work | and walks | takes a bus | Evan

_____

4 after 8:00 p.m. | does not eat | Joanna | or drink

_____

5 exercise a lot | we | and eat well

_____

6 Ms. Lee | yoga | and studies | teaches

_____

7 help the skin | healthy oils | and add weight

_____

8 tai chi | Sheila | and does | plays basketball

_____

2 Read each sentence in the chart. Write the verbs and the conjunction in the boxes in the correct columns.

	VERBS	CONJUNCTION
1. Felix loves coffee and drinks it every day.		
2. Danila does not eat meat or drink soda.		
3. They bought tea and gave me some.		
4. It is important to include a lot of water in your diet, and doctors recommend six glasses a day.		
5. Food can affect your health and how you learn.		
6. We do not eat or buy take-out food.		
7. Pam does not cook fish or eat it.		
8. Milk builds strong bones and helps your teeth.		
9. My father does not sleep well or eat properly.		
10. Connie does not drink or eat anything on Thursdays.		

D. Skill Quiz

Check (✓) the correct answer for each item.

1 What does a verb usually do?
   - ☐ a. It expresses an action.
   - ☐ b. It shows who is doing the action.
   - ☐ c. It joins two parts of a sentence.

2 Which words can join two verbs in a simple sentence?
   - ☐ a. for, so
   - ☐ b. and, or
   - ☐ c. with, together

3 In a simple sentence with two negative verbs, use *do not* or *does not*
   - ☐ a. only before the first verb.
   - ☐ b. before both verbs.
   - ☐ c. after both verbs.

4 Choose the verbs in this sentence: *I eat and drink healthy food.*
   - ☐ a. I, and
   - ☐ b. healthy, food
   - ☐ c. eat, drink

5 Choose the verb in this sentence: *Fish and nuts are a good source of oil.*
   - ☐ a. and
   - ☐ b. nuts
   - ☐ c. are

6 Choose the verbs in this sentence: *Some vegetarians do not drink milk or eat eggs.*
   - ☐ a. do not drink, eat
   - ☐ b. milk, eggs
   - ☐ c. some vegetarians, or

7 Choose the verb in this sentence: *Tea tastes good.*
   - ☐ a. tea
   - ☐ b. tastes
   - ☐ c. good

8 Choose the words that express what Taylor does not do: *Taylor does not sleep or eat well on the weekends.*
   - ☐ a. or, on
   - ☐ b. the, weekends
   - ☐ c. sleep, eat well

9 Choose the words that complete this sentence: *Green vegetables smell ___ good.*
   - ☐ a. and taste
   - ☐ b. are healthy
   - ☐ c. or fruit

10 Choose the words that complete this sentence: *I do not exercise ___ very much.*
   - ☐ a. and eat
   - ☐ b. or eat
   - ☐ c. eat or

Compound Sentences with *And*, *But*, and *So*

CONNECTING TO THE THEME

Are you a confident language learner?

Yes   No   I am fluent in one language, and I can have a conversation in at least one other language.

Yes   No   I learn new words easily, but I feel uncomfortable saying them out loud.

Yes   No   I like to practice new languages, so I got a conversation partner.

Mostly Yes: you're a confident language learner! Mostly No: you need some encouragement.

A. Skill Presentation

A compound sentence expresses at least two complete ideas. The ideas must be related to each other. The two ideas in a compound sentence are joined by a word called a conjunction. The **conjunction** explains the connection between the two ideas. Some conjunctions for compound sentences are *and*, *but*, and *so*.

And connects two similar ideas.

> People speak differently, **and** they use different words.

The idea of *speaking differently* and the idea of using *different words* are similar.

But connects two contrasting, or different, ideas.

> In Detroit they say *pop*, **but** in San Francisco they say *soda*.

Saying pop and *saying soda* are contrasting ideas.

So connects a cause and a result.

> Hugo grew up in the Northeast, **so** he says *soda*.

Growing up in the Northeast is the cause, and *saying soda* is the result. The reason that Hugo *says soda* is because he grew up in the Northeast.

B. Over to You

1 Read the paragraph. How many conjunctions are there? Circle them and check (✓) the correct answer.

Teenagers sometimes speak differently from adults, and they use special words. This helps teens feel unique, and it makes them feel independent. Some of these words are old, but others are very new. For example, teens first started saying *cool* in the 1940s, and they still say *cool* today. In the past, teens used other special words, but many of them are not used today. In the 1960s, teens said *groovy*, but they do not use that word now. Teenagers want to be unique, so they often use different words from adults.

☐ a. There are five conjunctions.
☐ b. There are seven conjunctions.
☐ c. There are ten conjunctions.

2 Match the two parts of the compound sentences.

1 *Pop* is a common word in Michigan,   ___ **a** and others call it *tonic*.

2 My aunt lived in Boston,   ___ **b** so I looked them up online.

3 Some people call cola *soda*,   ___ **c** and it comes from French.

4 *Ballet* is a borrowed word in English,   ___ **d** so many people understand it.

5 *Groovy* was used in the 1960s,   ___ **e** and sometimes I use a thesaurus.

6 *Bus* is an international word,   ___ **f** but it is rare in California.

7 I do not understand this word,   ___ **g** but now it is almost never used.

8 I could not find the definitions in the dictionary,   ___ **h** but I know how to pronounce it.

___ **i** so she says *tonic*.

9 Sometimes I use a dictionary,

CHECK!

1 A compound sentence expresses at least _____ complete ideas. The ideas must be _____ to each other.

2 The ideas can be connected with *and*, *but*, or *so*. _____ connects two similar ideas. _____ connects two contrasting ideas. _____ connects a cause and a result.

C. Practice

1 Read each sentence in the chart. Decide if the word in bold is a correct or incorrect conjunction. Check (✓) the box in the correct column.

	CORRECT CONJUNCTION	INCORRECT CONJUNCTION
1. English gives words to other languages, **and** other languages add words to English.		
2. I call this sandwich a *hero*, **so** my friend calls it a *hoagie*.		
3. English has many words from French, **so** it has some from German.		
4. We say *elevator* in the United States, **but** they say *lift* in England.		
5. I did not know the definition, **but** I used the dictionary.		
6. Americans say *stroller*, **but** they say *pram* in England.		
7. I say *you guys*, **so** my friends from the South say *y'all*.		
8. My roommates are learning English, **and** they are studying Chinese at school.		
9. I lived in the Midwest, **so** I use words that are common in that part of the country.		
10. *Bravo* is a foreign word, **and** we use it in English.		

2 Read each sentence and complete it with the correct conjunction (*and*, *but*, or *so*).

1 Some people speak fast, _____ they speak clearly.

2 He is from the South, _____ he says *y'all*.

3 Americans use different words, _____ they speak differently, too.

4 We wanted to see more of the city, _____ we didn't have time.

5 English has many words from other languages, _____ they are considered English words now.

6 Many French words are now international, _____ they are used all over the world.

7 Some words are common, _____ they are used in several languages.

8 People with a drawl stretch out the vowel sounds, _____ they speak more slowly.

9 *Origami* was originally a Japanese word, _____ it is now used in English, too.

10 Most people use abbreviations when they text, _____ they also use special words.

D. Skill Quiz

Check (✓) the correct answer for each item.

1 What connects two ideas in a compound sentence?

  ☐ a. a subject
  ☐ b. a verb
  ☐ c. a conjunction

2 The two ideas in a compound sentence

  ☐ a. must be related.
  ☐ b. must be true.
  ☐ c. must be incomplete.

3 A cause and a result are connected by

  ☐ a. *and.*
  ☐ b. *but.*
  ☐ c. *so.*

4 Contrasting ideas are connected by

  ☐ a. *and.*
  ☐ b. *but.*
  ☐ c. *so.*

5 Choose the correct answer to complete this compound sentence: Taxi *is an international word*, ___.

  ☐ a. and it is used all over the world
  ☐ b. and there are no taxis in my town
  ☐ c. and I own a car

6 Choose the correct answer to complete this compound sentence: *I use a dictionary to look up new words*, ___.

  ☐ a. but I finish my homework on time
  ☐ b. but the dictionary gives their definitions
  ☐ c. but I look up other information online

7 Choose the correct answer to complete this compound sentence: *In the United States, a television is called a* TV, ___.

  ☐ a. but I do not watch it very much
  ☐ b. but it is called a *telly* in England
  ☐ c. but English exports many words

8 Choose the correct answer to complete this compound sentence: *Some English learners already know Spanish*, ___.

  ☐ a. and I took French last semester
  ☐ b. so they can easily understand English words like *avocado* and *patio*
  ☐ c. but the word *patio* comes from Spanish

9 Choose the correct answer to complete this compound sentence: *A common phrase for* yard sale *is* garage sale, ___.

  ☐ a. and some houses have nice yards
  ☐ b. so *garage* is originally French
  ☐ c. but some people call it a *tag sale*

10 Choose the correct answer to complete this compound sentence: *The words* sofa *and* couch *are both common in North America*, ___.

  ☐ a. and British people use the word *Chesterfield* to describe one kind of sofa
  ☐ b. so many Americans say either word to mean the same thing
  ☐ c. but some people decide to buy chairs instead

There is and There are

Connecting to the Theme

Do you like changes or taking risks?[1]

There is a new job at your company, with much more responsibility than you have now. Would you apply?
  A no   **B** yes

There are new student insurance plans for stolen items. Would you buy one?
  A yes   **B** no

There is a perfect program at a university in a different country, but you do not speak the language. Would you apply?
  A no   **B** yes

Mostly As: you really don't like changes in your life or taking risks. Mostly Bs: you are happy to take risks.

A. Skill Presentation

Use the expressions *there is* and *there are* to introduce new information in your writing. *There is* is followed by a **singular noun**.

> There is a good **book** about starting a new job.

There are is followed by a **plural noun**.

> There are some helpful **tips** about working for a new company.

Use *there is* or *there are* at the beginning of a statement. They show that you are going to write about something you have not mentioned before. They introduce new information.

> I like working at this company. There are many friendly people.

The writer uses *there are* to introduce new information – the fact that *many friendly people* work at the company. When you write, use *there is* or *there are* only the first time you mention something.

> I like working at this company. There are many friendly people. They help me learn new things.

The writer used *there are* to introduce new information, and then the writer used the word *they* to refer to *many friendly people*. The writer did not use *there are* again to talk about *friendly people*. Remember, you cannot start a statement with *are*, *is*, *have*, or *has*. You must use the word *there*.

....

[1]**risk:** something you do that could cause danger or loss

B. Over to You

1   Complete the sentences with *There is* or *There are*.

1 _____ a great job opportunity in New York.

2 _____ many applicants.

3 _____ a pay increase.

4 _____ 58 employees at the company.

5 _____ two offices in London.

6 _____ three interviews for the position.

7 _____ one person who interviews each candidate.

8 _____ health benefits and retirement benefits.

9 _____ one day left to apply.

10 _____ several other jobs that I will apply for.

2   Circle the correct answer for each item.

1 There is *something | some things* I want to tell you. You know how untidy I am. Well, I am going to be tidy in future!

2 I need help getting organized. There are *too many appointments | only one appointment* to remember.

3 There is a *software program | software programs* in my electronic planner. It sends me an e-mail when I have an appointment.

4 There are *websites | a website* to help me stay organized.

5 There are *so many papers | one paper* around my apartment. I am going to throw most of them away.

6 I want to save money. There is *a utility plan | utilities plans* that is less expensive.

7 I am getting rid of some old clothes. There are *many shirts | a shirt* that I don't wear anymore.

8 There is *a local company | some local companies* that will pick up old clothes from my apartment.

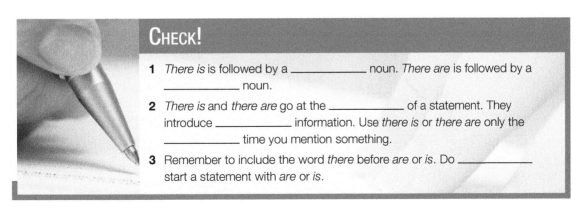

CHECK!

1 *There is* is followed by a _____ noun. *There are* is followed by a _____ noun.

2 *There is* and *there are* go at the _____ of a statement. They introduce _____ information. Use *there is* or *there are* only the _____ time you mention something.

3 Remember to include the word *there* before *are* or *is*. Do _____ start a statement with *are* or *is*.

C. Practice

1 Read the paragraph. How many sentences have mistakes? Check (✓) the correct answer.

¹There is a nice apartment building nearby. ²Has one large parking lot. ³There is also a laundry room in the basement. ⁴The laundry room is very large. ⁵Are a few apartments available in the building. ⁶There is a two-bedroom apartment on the second floor. ⁷The two-bedroom apartment has a big kitchen. ⁸There is a three-bedroom apartment on the fourth floor. ⁹Is more space in this apartment. ¹⁰We want to move soon. ¹¹Are many details we have to think about first.

☐   a. Four sentences have mistakes. Sentences: _____
☐   b. Five sentences have mistakes. Sentences: _____
☐   c. Six sentences have mistakes. Sentences: _____

2 Read each item in the chart. Check (✓) the box in the correct column to complete it.

	THERE IS	THERE ARE
1. Leaving your job can be scary. ___ risks that you need to consider.		
2. I found some useful information. ___ a website about how to dress at work.		
3. ___ a lot of bills for us to pay this month as well as the rent.		
4. As we need more staff, ___ three new employees starting next Monday.		
5. ___ more space in our new apartment than our old one.		
6. My brother has many challenges at work, but he says ___ always a solution to every problem.		
7. They are a good company to work for. ___ many benefits apart from a good salary.		
8. ___ many factors to take into consideration when changing your job.		
9. ___ a small apartment for sale on the next block.		
10. ___ two closets in the main bedroom and one in the spare bedroom.		

D. Skill Quiz

Check (✓) the correct answer for each item.

1 The expressions *There is* and *There are*
   - ☐ a. repeat information.
   - ☐ b. give useless information.
   - ☐ c. introduce new information.

2 *There is* is always followed by a
   - ☐ a. singular noun.
   - ☐ b. plural noun.
   - ☐ c. proper noun.

3 *There are* is always followed by a
   - ☐ a. singular noun.
   - ☐ b. plural noun.
   - ☐ c. proper noun.

4 Choose the correct sentence.
   - ☐ a. There is a job opening at my office.
   - ☐ b. There are a job opening at my office.
   - ☐ c. Has a job opening at my office.

5 Choose the correct sentence.
   - ☐ a. Are 50 employees at the company.
   - ☐ b. There is 50 employees at the company.
   - ☐ c. There are 50 employees at the company.

6 Choose the correct sentence.
   - ☐ a. There is an insurance plan for employees.
   - ☐ b. Have an insurance plan for employees.
   - ☐ c. There are an insurance plan for employees.

7 Choose the correct sentence.
   - ☐ a. There is a new house for sale in the neighborhood.
   - ☐ b. There are a new house for sale in the neighborhood.
   - ☐ c. Is a new house for sale in the neighborhood.

8 Choose the correct sentence.
   - ☐ a. There are a closet in the bedroom.
   - ☐ b. There is one closet in the hall.
   - ☐ c. There is four bedrooms and two closets.

9 Choose the correct sentence.
   - ☐ a. There is some good professors at my school.
   - ☐ b. There is many classes that interest me.
   - ☐ c. There is a program that interests me.

10 Choose the correct sentence.
   - ☐ a. There are a scholarship for some students.
   - ☐ b. There are scholarships for students who work full time.
   - ☐ c. There are one scholarship for the best student athlete.

MEALS AROUND THE WORLD

CONNECTING TO THE THEME

Which dishes from around the world have you tried?

Have you ever tried biryani, a spicy dish from India?

  A Yes! I like food that tastes hot.   **B** Yes, but I didn't like it.   **C** I've never tried it.

Have you ever tried coffee from Turkey?

  A Yes! I like strong coffee.   **B** Yes, but I don't like it –   **C** I've never tried it.
                                                  the flavor is too powerful.

Have you ever had baklava, a dessert typical, or common, in the Middle East?

  A Yes, and I liked it! I like   **B** Yes, but it was too sweet   **C** I've never tried it.
    sweet food.   for me.

Mostly As: you are very open to new foods. Mostly Bs: you try new things, but you don't like many flavors.
Mostly Cs: you need to try new things!

A. Skill Presentation

Remember that nouns can be the names of people, places, or things, or they can be ideas. All sentences have at least one noun.

Remember that verbs usually express **action**. They express what a noun does. Some verbs are **non-action** verbs. They can show that a noun belongs to someone, or they can express a quality a person has. All sentences have at least one verb.

ACTION VERBS	**NON-ACTION VERBS**
eat, celebrate, give	be, have, like

Adjectives describe nouns. Use adjectives when you write to give details about a person, place, thing, or idea. Adjectives create a more complete picture for your reader.

Carlos is **hungry**.   We ate at a **nice** restaurant.

The oranges are **sweet**.   Linda had a **good** time at lunch.

B. Over to You

1 **Read the sentences. Decide if the words in bold are nouns, verbs, or adjectives. Write each word in the correct column of the chart.**

The **coffee is strong**.
Julia likes a **big lunch**.
The **store has crusty bread**.
The **grapes are green**.
Marcos and Adriana eat typical food.

NOUNS	VERBS	ADJECTIVES

2 **Read the paragraph about birthday foods. How many adjectives are there? Circle them and check (✓) the correct answer.**

There are different foods for birthdays around the world. Cake is a typical food for birthdays. It is popular all over the world. In Cuba and Mexico, children have a big piñata. A piñata is a sort of doll filled with special candy. In India, children give delicious chocolates to their classmates. In Russia, people have pies on their birthdays. A wish is written on the crusty top. People eat their favorite treats around the world on their birthdays.

☐ a. There are four adjectives.
☐ b. There are eight adjectives.
☐ c. There are ten adjectives.

CHECK!

1 When you write, you must use _____ and _____ .

2 You can also use _____ . Use adjectives to describe _____ .
They give details about people, _____ , things, and _____ to
help create a complete picture for your reader.

C. Practice

1 **Choose the correct adjective to complete each sentence.**

big   **popular**   **good**   **hard**   **typical**   **hungry**   **crowded**   **spicy**

1 My brothers are _____. They did not eat breakfast.

2 Noodles are a _____ dish in China. Almost everyone eats them.

3 These tacos have a _____ flavor. They are too hot for me.

4 This is a _____ restaurant. It has room for 200 people.

5 Did you have a _____ time at the New Year's party?

6 Ralph is not a _____ teenager. He hates pizza!

7 We went to a _____ café, and we had to wait an hour to sit down.

8 That was _____ work. Now we need to eat!

2 **Read each sentence in the chart. Write the noun, verb, and adjective in the box in the correct column.**

	NOUN	VERB	ADJECTIVE
1. The bread is crusty.			
2. The chicken had a spicy flavor.			
3. We ate at a typical café.			
4. I like my coffee strong.			
5. We eat a big breakfast every morning.			
6. Jan likes hot cereal in the mornings.			
7. We only have a light meal in the evenings.			
8. I drank some warm milk.			
9. These grapes are sweet.			
10. They had a nice dinner.			

D. Skill Quiz

Check (✓) the correct answer for each item.

1 What is a noun?
- ☐ a. the name of a person, place, thing, or idea
- ☐ b. a word that describes a verb
- ☐ c. a word that expresses an action

2 What is a verb?
- ☐ a. the name of a person, place, or thing, or an idea
- ☐ b. a word that describes an adjective
- ☐ c. a word that expresses an action

3 What is an adjective?
- ☐ a. the name of a person, place, thing, or idea
- ☐ b. a word that describes a noun
- ☐ c. a word that expresses an action

4 Adjectives can help
- ☐ a. show your reader who or what is doing the action.
- ☐ b. give details to help create a complete picture for your reader.
- ☐ c. show your reader in what direction a thing is moving.

5 Choose the adjective in this sentence: *I like strong tea.*
- ☐ a. like
- ☐ b. strong
- ☐ c. tea

6 Choose the adjective in this sentence: *The bread is crusty.*
- ☐ a. bread
- ☐ b. is
- ☐ c. crusty

7 Choose the adjective in this sentence: *New Year's Eve is an exciting holiday.*
- ☐ a. is
- ☐ b. exciting
- ☐ c. holiday

8 Choose the word that completes this sentence: *We have a ___ lunch with friends.*
- ☐ a. big
- ☐ b. meal
- ☐ c. eat

9 Choose the word that completes this sentence: *That dish is ___.*
- ☐ a. tastes
- ☐ b. meal
- ☐ c. spicy

10 Choose the word that completes this sentence: *John is ___.*
- ☐ a. lunch
- ☐ b. eats
- ☐ c. hungry

20

Review: Simple and Compound Sentences

SOCIAL CUSTOMS

CONNECTING TO THE THEME

How much do you know about social customs around the world? Are these statements true or false?

1 In most countries, it is polite to talk with your mouth full of food.

2 You are invited to dinner at 8:00 p.m., so it is polite to arrive at 9:00 p.m.

3 You meet an American for the first time. It is polite to shake hands and smile.

4 You meet a business partner in Japan, and you want to be polite. You bow to your partner and you hand him a business card with both hands.

1 False (it is not polite to talk with your mouth full in most countries), 2 False (it is polite to arrive on time for dinner), 3 True, 4 True.

A. Skill Presentation

A **simple sentence** has one subject–verb group, and it expresses one complete idea.

> **I brought** flowers to Rodrigo.

> **We danced** and **sang**.

A **compound sentence** has at least two subject–verb groups, and it expresses at least two complete ideas. These ideas must be related.

> **Sandra and I liked** the flowers, **and Camilo enjoyed** the chocolates.

In a compound sentence, two complete ideas are joined by a **conjunction**. Some common conjunctions are *and*, *but*, and *so*. *And* connects similar ideas, *but* connects contrasting ideas, and *so* connects a cause with its result. When you write, put a comma before the conjunction.

B. Over to You

1 **Read the paragraph. How many compound sentences are there? Check (✓) the correct answer.**

¹Adae started a new job in the United States last year. ²She learned many new customs. ³People shake hands when they meet, and they make eye contact. ⁴People often call each other by their first names. ⁵On Fridays, the people in her office dress casually. ⁶Today is Friday, but Adae forgot. ⁷She is wearing a suit. ⁸There is a meeting today. ⁹Adae wants to be polite, so she arrives at the meeting early. ¹⁰There is a new employee at the meeting. ¹¹The new employee is from a different country, so Adae will give her some helpful tips.

☐ a. There are three compound sentences. Sentences: _____

☐ b. There are four compound sentences. Sentences: _____

☐ c. There are five compound sentences. Sentences: _____

2 **Read each sentence in the chart. Decide if it is a simple or compound sentence. Check (✓) the box in the correct column.**

	SIMPLE SENTENCE	COMPOUND SENTENCE
1. Luciana brought roses to the dinner party.		
2. Wei gave her host a small present.		
3. Chang bowed, and Michael introduced him.		
4. Pedro is traveling to China, so Martin is teaching him Chinese.		
5. Megan does not put her arms on the dinner table.		
6. Martin is going to the party, but Hana is staying at home.		
7. In South Korea, many people wrap gifts in red or yellow paper.		
8. Lily wanted to be polite, so she took chocolates to her host.		
9. Jin is bringing roses to the host, and Jorge is bringing a plant.		
10. Daniel invited his friends to a dinner party.		

CHECK!

1 A simple sentence has one _____–_____ group, and it expresses one complete idea.

2 A compound sentence has at least _____ subject–verb groups. It expresses at least two complete ideas that are _____.

3 Remember to use the correct _____ and a _____ when you write compound sentences.

C. Practice

1 Check (✓) the correct answer for each item.

1 Choose the compound sentence.

☐ a. In Lebanon, people bring a dessert to a dinner party.

☐ b. Rashid lives in Lebanon and works for a large company.

☐ c. Rashid likes dessert, so Mariam gave him a cake.

2 Choose the simple sentence.

☐ a. In Russia, the host serves the oldest guest first.

☐ b. Tanya's grandfather is the oldest, so Anton will serve him first.

☐ c. Tanya's grandfather is 72, and Tanya is 23.

4 Choose the compound sentence.

☐ a. Adriana took a cake to the party, and Pablo took soda.

☐ b. Pablo brought soda to the party for Adriana.

☐ c. Adriana and Pablo ate cake and talked at the party.

5 Choose the simple sentence.

☐ a. Mariela wants to eat at a restaurant, but her friends want to cook.

☐ b. Mariela prefers Italian food to French food, and her friends like it, too.

☐ c. Mariela's friends want to cook dinner together.

6 Choose the compound sentence.

☐ a. Antonio smiled, and Ravi said, "Good morning."

☐ b. Antonio said good morning to his neighbor.

☐ c. Antonio smiled and talked with his neighbor.

7 Choose the simple sentence.

☐ a. Ronaldo speaks Chinese, but Clara only speaks English.

☐ b. Ronaldo and Clara studied English and computer science.

☐ c. Ronaldo finished college, so he does not have classes with Clara.

2 Read the paragraph and answer the questions.

¹Crystal visited Colombia last year, so she learned many new customs. ²She was invited to someone's home for dinner, and she had a very enjoyable evening. ³Crystal brought some flowers with her. ⁴She shook hands with her host. ⁵She said "Good evening." ⁶Her host told her where to sit at the table. ⁷She tried all the food, but Crystal left a small amount of food on her plate to be polite. ⁸She stayed for two hours after dinner. ⁹It is not polite to "eat and run." ¹⁰Her Colombian hosts were happy they invited her, and Crystal was happy she went.

1 How many simple sentences does the text have? ___ Sentences: _____

2 How many compound sentences does the text have? ___ Sentences: _____

3 What conjunctions are used? _____

4 Are commas used before the conjunctions? _____

D. Skill Quiz

Check (✓) the correct answer for each item.

1 A simple sentence always has
  ☐ a. a subject, a verb, and two complete ideas.
  ☐ b. two subjects, two verbs, and one complete idea.
  ☐ c. a subject and a verb.

2 A compound sentence always has
  ☐ a. two subjects and two verbs.
  ☐ b. two subjects and one verb.
  ☐ c. one subject and one verb.

3 A compound sentence always has
  ☐ a. a preposition.
  ☐ b. an adverb.
  ☐ c. a conjunction.

4 Some examples of conjunctions are
  ☐ a. *and*, *so*, and *but*.
  ☐ b. *from*, *between*, and *into*.
  ☐ c. *while*, *during*, and *until*.

5 Choose the simple sentence.
  ☐ a. Mr. Bertolini hosted a dinner party on Sunday.
  ☐ b. Mr. Bertolini hosted a party, so Daniela brought roses.
  ☐ c. Mr. Bertolini hosted a party, but Paolo did not come.

6 Choose the simple sentence.
  ☐ a. Nguyen moved to the United States, and Pia taught him the customs.
  ☐ b. Nguyen and Pia traveled to the United States together last month.
  ☐ c. Nguyen went to the United States, but he did not speak English.

7 Choose the simple sentence.
  ☐ a. Henry was late for the party, but Elizabeth was on time.
  ☐ b. Elizabeth was late for the party, so she apologized.
  ☐ c. Henry brought a box of chocolates to the party.

8 Choose the compound sentence.
  ☐ a. Pedro is from Chile, and Anna is from Argentina.
  ☐ b. Pedro speaks Spanish and English.
  ☐ c. Anna moved from Argentina to Chile.

9 Choose the compound sentence.
  ☐ a. Kenna visited her family's friends in Colombia.
  ☐ b. Kenna learned Spanish, so she understood her Colombian hosts.
  ☐ c. Kenna learned Spanish at a school in Colombia.

10 Choose the compound sentence.
  ☐ a. Dianne loves Vietnamese food, so she is taking a Vietnamese cooking class.
  ☐ b. Dianne wants to learn how to cook Vietnamese food.
  ☐ c. Dianne loves to learn new things and take classes.

Review: Topic, Supporting, and Concluding Sentences

CONNECTING TO THE THEME

How do you connect with other people?

- instant messenger services
- personal blog
- video calls
- video-sharing website
- text messages

- social networking site
- e-mails
- telephone calls
- online games
- photo-sharing website

1–3 items: you prefer to connect with people face-to-face. 4–6 items: you connect with people in many different ways. 7–10 items: you should try to communicate more with people face-to-face.

A. Skill Presentation

A paragraph has several parts. The **topic sentence** tells the main idea of a paragraph. There is only one topic sentence in a paragraph.

Supporting sentences give more information about the topic sentence. There are several supporting sentences in a paragraph.

The **concluding sentence** can repeat the main idea of the paragraph using different words. It is usually the last sentence in a paragraph. There is only one concluding sentence in a paragraph.

> [T]I like keeping in touch with my friends online. [S]My online phone service is easy to use. [S]It does not cost a lot of money. [C]I really enjoy communicating with friends over the Internet.

This paragraph gives us more information about why the writer likes to keep in touch with friends online.

B. Over to You

1 Read the paragraphs. Write the sentence numbers in the correct columns in the chart.

1   ¹Video-sharing websites are very popular. ²Anyone can post videos online. ³People all over the world can see them. ⁴Many people use these websites to share videos with others.

2   ⁵Staying connected is important to many students. ⁶They use their cell phones to call and text. ⁷Social networking sites help these students stay in touch with friends. ⁸These connections are a big part of their lives.

	TOPIC SENTENCE	SUPPORTING SENTENCES	CONCLUDING SENTENCE
1			
2			

2 Read the paragraphs. The sentence in bold is not in the correct place. Decide if it should be the topic sentence, a supporting sentence, or the concluding sentence. Check (✓) the box in the correct column.

Paragraph 1
People can simply type a message and click "send." Texting is a popular way for people to communicate. They can keep in touch with many people this way. Sending messages like this is one way for people to stay in touch.

Paragraph 2
We can log on to review assignments. **Our professor keeps a helpful blog for our class.** We can also read summaries of class lectures. This blog makes it easy to know what is happening in class.

	TOPIC SENTENCE	SUPPORTING SENTENCE	CONCLUDING SENTENCE
1			
2			

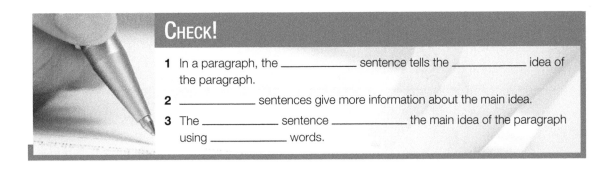

CHECK!

1 In a paragraph, the _____ sentence tells the _____ idea of the paragraph.

2 _____ sentences give more information about the main idea.

3 The _____ sentence _____ the main idea of the paragraph using _____ words.

C. Practice

1 Read the paragraphs and check (✓) the correct answers.

1   Now you can share a book with a child far away. There is a website with online children's books. You can connect with a child by video call and read a book together. ___

Choose the correct concluding sentence for this paragraph.

☐ a. Grandparents can read to their grandchildren on a website.
☐ b. Now you can enjoy story time with a child from anywhere in the world.
☐ c. Sharing books with your friends is an enjoyable thing to do.

2   ___ He puts the pictures on a social networking site. He writes comments under each photo. It is fun for Paul to post his travel experiences online.

Choose the correct topic sentence for this paragraph.

☐ a. Paul likes sharing his vacation photographs with friends.
☐ b. Paul got a new computer last year.
☐ c. Paul was not able to take a vacation this year.

2 Match each topic sentence (1–5) with two correct supporting sentences (a–h).

1 Internet communication companies let people communicate in different ways.   ___   ___

2 The critic's comments about the movie were helpful.   ___   ___

3 The band has a blog about what they are doing.   ___   ___

4 These days, not many people communicate by writing letters.   ___   ___

5 We can order pizza online.   ___   ___

a People read it to find out where they are playing.

b We just have to enter some information and click the button that says "Order now."

c You can text or make voice calls.

d You can also make video calls.

e They e-mail or call instead.

f You can also buy tickets for their concerts.

g They also send text messages.

h He said the actors were good, but the story was not.

i It even tells you what time it will be delivered.

j He also said the special effects were excellent.

D. Skill Quiz

Check (✓)the correct answer for each item.

1 The three main parts of a paragraph are
- ☐ a. a topic sentence, supporting sentences, and a concluding sentence.
- ☐ b. two supporting sentences and a concluding sentence.
- ☐ c. a topic sentence and two supporting sentences.

2 A topic sentence
- ☐ a. gives examples related to the main idea of a paragraph.
- ☐ b. tells the main idea of a paragraph.
- ☐ c. repeats the main idea of a paragraph using different words.

3 Supporting sentences
- ☐ a. repeat the main idea of a paragraph.
- ☐ b. give more information about the topic sentence.
- ☐ c. always come at the end of the paragraph.

4 A concluding sentence
- ☐ a. can repeat the topic sentence exactly.
- ☐ b. can introduce the main idea for the first time.
- ☐ c. can repeat the topic sentence using different words.

5 Which is a good topic sentence for a paragraph about the many uses of cell phones?
- ☐ a. Cell phones can be expensive.
- ☐ b. Some people still prefer to use a regular camera.
- ☐ c. There are a lot of things that cell phones can do.

6 Which is a good topic sentence for a paragraph about how to send a text?
- ☐ a. Please do not text in class.
- ☐ b. To send a text, just type and click.
- ☐ c. Calling is easier than sending a text.

7 Choose the correct supporting sentence for this topic sentence: *Online phone services let people communicate in two ways.*
- ☐ a. One way is to make a video call.
- ☐ b. The service is not expensive.
- ☐ c. Regular phones are still popular.

8 Choose the correct supporting sentence for this topic sentence: *Video calls let you see the person you are calling.*
- ☐ a. Texting is a good way to stay in touch.
- ☐ b. An image appears on your computer screen.
- ☐ c. Some online games are easy to use.

9 Choose the correct supporting sentence for this topic sentence: *Many people enjoy sharing pictures on the computer.*
- ☐ a. Sending photos online is fun for a lot of people.
- ☐ b. Many websites offer free e-mail.
- ☐ c. Some people spend too much time online.

10 Choose the correct supporting sentence for this topic sentence: *There is a popular website where people post messages.*
- ☐ a. The messages are about everyday news.
- ☐ b. Messages on this website have to be short.
- ☐ c. This website allows many people to share comments online.

Recognizing Irrelevant Sentences

COLLEGE LIFE

CONNECTING TO THE THEME

What are some benefits of going to college?

- getting qualifications to get a good job
- developing leadership skills
- meeting advisers who give you good advice about classes and careers
- gaining a clearer idea of career goals
- meeting more people from other cultures
- gaining confidence and independence
- improving communication skills

All the items are likely benefits of going to college.

A. Skill Presentation

Remember that supporting sentences in a paragraph are **directly related** to the main idea in the **topic sentence. Irrelevant** sentences are sentences in a paragraph that do not relate to the main idea. Do not include them in your writing. They may confuse your reader. Look at this example.

> [TS]You may need help with financial problems in college. For financial issues, contact the financial aid office. Someone in the office can answer financial questions.

Both of the supporting sentences above relate to the main idea.

Now look at this example.

> [TS]You may need help with financial problems in college. Tutors can help you study. Visit a university before you decide to go there. ✗

These sentences are not good supporting sentences because they do not relate to the main idea. They are not about financial problems in college – they are irrelevant. Do not include irrelevant sentences in your writing.

B. Over to You

1 **Read the topic sentence. Then read each sentence in the chart and decide if it is related to the main idea or not. Check (✓) the box in the correct column.**

Topic Sentence: Teaching assistants (TAs) do many things to help college professors and students.

	RELATES	DOES NOT RELATE
1. Professors earn money for their work.		
2. TAs meet with students to discuss issues with homework.		
3. TAs often prepare materials for class.		
4. My TA is extremely well educated.		
5. Some TAs teach courses for the professor.		
6. Some students receive help from family members.		

2 **Read each topic sentence. Check (✓) the supporting sentence that most closely relates to the main idea.**

1 You should have several goals when you are in college.
- ☐ a. Set short-term and long-term goals for the year.
- ☐ b. Ask your friends what their plans are for the weekend.

2 The Department of Languages has several new majors.
- ☐ a. The Department of Science offers biology and chemistry classes.
- ☐ b. They are now offering majors in Chinese and Korean.

3 There are some typical problems that many students have.
- ☐ a. Students can have personal difficulties that affect their academic work.
- ☐ b. Advisers often give students information about new courses.

4 There are many things you should do before choosing a school.
- ☐ a. Start paying back your student loans.
- ☐ b. Research colleges online, and talk to people you know about the colleges.

CHECK!

1 When you write a _____, be sure all of the _____ sentences _____ to your main idea.

2 _____ sentences do not relate to the main idea. Do not _____ them in your writing.

C. Practice

1 Read each topic sentence. Check (✓) the supporting sentence that does not relate to the main idea.

1 A financial adviser can answer questions about money.

☐ a. A financial adviser can help you find ways to pay for your classes.
☐ b. If you don't know where to get money, a financial adviser can help.
☐ c. Some counselors offer help for personal problems.

2 Ms. Lynch suggested I get a tutor to help me with my pronunciation.

☐ a. Her idea is that I watch more movies on TV.
☐ b. She thinks working with one person will help me a lot.
☐ c. We can focus on where I really have problems.

3 Most of my classes are in the English department.

☐ a. My professors' offices are there, too.
☐ b. A lot of my friends are in this department.
☐ c. So is the financial adviser.

4 I am dealing with a difficult issue right now.

☐ a. My roommate always wants to watch TV when I need to study.
☐ b. She turns the volume up really high.
☐ c. We both enjoy the same programs, though.

5 I think it will help if I discuss the problem with someone.

☐ a. We always have dinner together in the evening.
☐ b. I will talk to my parents about it tonight.
☐ c. They always have good advice.

6 I talked to my adviser about some problems I was having in my classes.

☐ a. Her suggestions about how to get better grades were helpful.
☐ b. She told me how to get financial aid or even a scholarship.
☐ c. She also gave me some good advice about how to study.

2 Read the paragraph. How many irrelevant sentences are there? Check (✓) the correct answer.

[1]An academic adviser is a person who can help with decisions about school. [2]There are many ways your adviser can help. [3]It is a good idea to get your adviser's advice before you choose a major. [4]Talk to your adviser about the classes that interest you. [5]Be sure to tell your adviser about your favorite social activities. [6]Your adviser can also help you if you are having trouble in a course. [7]Many students' parents care about their children's personal problems. [8]Your adviser may also show you websites with tips about how to succeed in school. [9]You may be able to find out personal information about your teachers online, too. [10]An adviser can also help you with questions like "How many classes should I take each semester?" [11]It is important to speak with your adviser about any academic issues you have.

☐ a. There are three irrelevant sentences. Sentences: _____
☐ b. There are four irrelevant sentences. Sentences: _____
☐ c. There are six irrelevant sentences. Sentences: _____

D. Skill Quiz

Check (✓) the correct answer for each item.

1 A good supporting sentence
   - ☐ a. is irrelevant.
   - ☐ b. relates to the main idea.
   - ☐ c. does not belong in a paragraph.

2 An irrelevant sentence
   - ☐ a. supports the topic sentence.
   - ☐ b. relates to the main idea.
   - ☐ c. does not relate to the main idea.

3 Do not include irrelevant sentences in your writing because
   - ☐ a. they may confuse your reader.
   - ☐ b. they are not grammatically correct.
   - ☐ c. they will probably make your paragraph too short.

4 Which kind of information is irrelevant in a paragraph about financial aid?
   - ☐ a. organizations that help with financial aid
   - ☐ b. how many hours teachers work
   - ☐ c. how much it costs to go to a college

5 Which kind of information is irrelevant in a paragraph about majors at a college?
   - ☐ a. how popular different majors are
   - ☐ b. what classes to take in high school
   - ☐ c. descriptions of the majors offered

6 Which sentence is irrelevant in a paragraph about sleeping habits?
   - ☐ a. There are often sales for beds online.
   - ☐ b. Most people need about eight hours of sleep.
   - ☐ c. College students often sleep less than they should.

7 Which sentence is irrelevant in a paragraph about time management?
   - ☐ a. Making a to-do list can help you manage your time.
   - ☐ b. It can take several weeks or months to find a job.
   - ☐ c. Limit time on the Internet that is not for work or school.

8 Which sentence is irrelevant in a paragraph about a tutoring service?
   - ☐ a. The tutors help people with many different subjects.
   - ☐ b. Tutors spend several hours with each student every month.
   - ☐ c. Some schools offer more financial aid than others.

9 Which question is irrelevant in a paragraph about reaching goals?
   - ☐ a. Where does the word *reach* come from originally?
   - ☐ b. How long will it take to accomplish my goal?
   - ☐ c. How many goals should I set at one time?

10 Which question is irrelevant in a paragraph about a college?
   - ☐ a. Where can I find a better job?
   - ☐ b. How many academic departments are there?
   - ☐ c. How much does each class cost?

23

Complex Sentences

CONNECTING TO THE THEME

How much do you know about body language?

Body language is movements that show other people your feelings without words. Which group is believed to be better at recognizing body language?

A men   **B** women   **C** neither

Which of the following is a sign that someone is telling a lie?

A crossing their legs   **B** looking down   **C** scratching their head

Is eye contact polite in every country?

A yes   **B** no   **C** not sure

Mostly As: you need to learn about body language. Mostly Bs: you know a lot about people's body language. Mostly Cs: you are often confused by other people's body language.

A. Skill Presentation

A **complex sentence** has two parts. An independent clause is one part of a complex sentence. It has a subject and a verb, and it expresses one complete idea. A dependent clause is the other part of a complex sentence. It has a subject and a verb, but it does not express a complete idea. A dependent clause needs an independent clause to make a complete idea. When you join a dependent clause and an independent clause, you make a complex sentence.

— INDEPENDENT CLAUSE — ——— DEPENDENT CLAUSE ———
Abdul travels quite a lot because he is a businessman.

In this sentence, the first part is the independent clause. *Abdul* is the subject, *travels* is the verb, and there is one complete idea. The second part is the dependent clause. There is information missing – we do not know what happens because he is a businessman.

A dependent clause always begins with a **conjunction**. You can use the conjunctions *because*, *if*, and *when* with dependent clauses.

Greg learned Turkish customs **because** he works in Turkey.

Jim will spend more time in Istanbul **if** he travels to Turkey again.

Rima follows Turkish customs **when** she visits Turkey.

B. Over to You

1 **Read each clause in the chart. Decide if it is independent or dependent. Check (✓) the box in the correct column.**

	INDEPENDENT CLAUSE	DEPENDENT CLAUSE
1. Because he is in a meeting		
2. When she visited China		
3. Paolo speaks Portuguese and Russian		
4. Jin shakes Natalia's hand		
5. Because her mother is from Quebec		
6. Because it shows bad manners		
7. Abena nods her head		
8. If he does not understand		

2 **Check (✓) the complex sentence in each item.**

1 ☐ a. Paula looked at Ana.
☐ b. Paula looked at Ana, but Ana did not look at Paula.
☐ c. Paula and Ana looked at each other when they met.

2 ☐ a. Ana studied Spanish, but Tomas studied French.
☐ b. Ana met Tomas when they were in college.
☐ c. Ana studied Spanish and spoke it in Ecuador.

3 ☐ a. Carlo felt guilty, so he crossed his arms.
☐ b. Carlo and Tina argued today.
☐ c. Carlo is sad because he argued with Tina.

4 ☐ a. Antonio bowed to Kazuo when they met.
☐ b. Antonio and Kazuo bowed to each other.
☐ c. Antonio introduced himself, and Kazuo bowed.

5 ☐ a. Marisa and Ken shook hands at the meeting.
☐ b. Marisa shook Ken's hand, and he introduced himself.
☐ c. Marisa shook hands with Ken when they met.

CHECK!

1 A _____ sentence has an independent clause and a dependent clause joined by a _____ such as *because*, *if*, or *when*.

2 Both _____ have a subject and a verb, but a dependent clause does not _____ a complete idea. An independent clause expresses a complete idea.

C. Practice

1 A Underline the dependent clause in each complex sentence.

1 People should learn Turkish customs if they want to work in Turkey.

2 Jim learns new customs when he travels.

3 I didn't like the movie because I didn't like the message in it.

4 Face-to-face conversations are usually clearer because it is easier to tell if someone doesn't understand you.

5 Your listener will relax if you smile when you talk.

B Now underline the independent clause in each complex sentence.

6 Many people make gestures with their hands when they speak.

7 It is important to learn about the local customs when you do business.

8 Body language is an important part of any conversation because people often respond to what you do more than to what you say.

9 In job interviews, it is important to look directly at interviewers if you want them to trust you.

10 Remember that communication is not just speaking because your eyes, hands, and body also "say" a lot.

2 Read the text. How many complex sentences are there? Check (✓) the correct answer.

¹Pedro will move to Vietnam if he finds a job there. ²Now he is trying to learn more about Vietnamese culture. ³He attends Vietnamese language classes three times a week. ⁴He is also reading a book about Vietnamese business customs. According to the book:

- ⁵He should bring a small gift to business meetings.
- ⁶He should shake hands with people when he meets them.
- ⁷He should hold his business card in both hands when he gives it to someone.
- ⁸He should make appointments in advance.
- ⁹He should get to know people first if he wants to build business relationships with them.
- ¹⁰It will be easier to meet new people if he makes contacts before he goes to Vietnam.
- ¹¹He should learn at least a few words of Vietnamese.
- ¹²He should never point at another person in Vietnam.

☐ a. There are two complex sentences. Sentences: _____
☐ b. There are three complex sentences. Sentences: _____
☐ c. There are five complex sentences. Sentences: _____

D. Skill Quiz

Check (✓) the correct answer for each item.

1 An independent clause
- [ ] a. has a conjunction and either a subject or a verb.
- [ ] b. is a complete idea and has a subject and a verb.
- [ ] c. is not a complete idea but has a subject and a verb.

2 A dependent clause
- [ ] a. has a conjunction and either a subject or a verb.
- [ ] b. is a complete idea and has a subject and a verb.
- [ ] c. is not a complete idea but has a subject and a verb.

3 A complex sentence has
- [ ] a. an independent clause and a dependent clause.
- [ ] b. two independent clauses and a conjunction.
- [ ] c. two dependent clauses.

4 Examples of conjunctions in complex sentences are
- [ ] a. *but, and,* and *or.*
- [ ] b. *when, because,* and *if.*
- [ ] c. *about, into,* and *through.*

5 Choose the complex sentence.
- [ ] a. Selin got a new job and wanted to learn Spanish.
- [ ] b. Selin learned Spanish because she moved to Chile.
- [ ] c. Selin speaks Spanish, and her co-workers speak it, as well.

6 Choose the complex sentence.
- [ ] a. Ryan studies business, and Carlo studies management.
- [ ] b. Ryan is studying business and engineering.
- [ ] c. Ryan will study management if he is accepted into the university.

7 Choose the complex sentence.
- [ ] a. Alejandro bowed to show respect.
- [ ] b. Alejandro bowed, so Wei did, too.
- [ ] c. Alejandro bowed to Wei when Wei bowed to him.

8 Choose the complex sentence.
- [ ] a. Stefania works in Italy, but Gerardo works in the United States.
- [ ] b. Stefania works in Italy because she speaks Italian.
- [ ] c. Stefania and Gerardo both speak English.

9 Choose the complex sentence.
- [ ] a. Anton stands close to his family and friends.
- [ ] b. Anton eats a lot when he is in Brazil.
- [ ] c. Anton is going to Brazil, so he is learning about Brazilian culture.

10 Choose the complex sentence.
- [ ] a. Yousef will speak Turkish if he moves to Turkey.
- [ ] b. Yousef and his family want to move to Turkey.
- [ ] c. Yousef likes Ankara, but his wife prefers Istanbul.

Sentences with *Because*

CONNECTING TO THE THEME

Do you know what they invented?

1 Mark Zuckerberg started developing this at Harvard University because students needed somewhere to post their photos and telephone numbers.
  A the World Wide Web   **B** a social network   **C** the cell phone

2 Tim Berners-Lee's invention happened because he wanted to share up-to-date information with other researchers.
  A the cell phone   **B** a social network   **C** the World Wide Web

3 Douglas Engelbart's invention was useful because it made a computer easier to use.
  A the elevator   **B** the computer mouse   **C** the World Wide Web

4 Dr. Martin Cooper's invention happened because he liked the Star Trek movies.
  A the computer mouse   **B** the elevator   **C** the cell phone

1B, 2C, 3B, 4C

A. Skill Presentation

An **independent clause** has a subject and a verb, and it expresses a complete idea. It can stand alone. All simple sentences are independent clauses.

> **People send** notes.

Because is a conjunction. Use the word *because* to explain why. *Because* begins a dependent clause. A **dependent clause** has a subject and a verb, but it does not express a complete idea.

> **because** it is easy

This is not a complete idea. We do not know what happens *because it is easy*. A dependent clause by itself is a sentence fragment. It needs an independent clause to make a complete idea.

> People send notes because it is easy.

This is a complete sentence. It has two clauses: one independent clause and one dependent clause with *because*.

B. Over to You

1 Read each item in the chart. Decide if it is a complete sentence or a sentence fragment. Check (✓) the box in the correct column.

	COMPLETE SENTENCE	SENTENCE FRAGMENT
1. Sam got a new cell phone because his phone broke		
2. Because they talk to friends		
3. New phones are useful because they can do many things		
4. The company was successful because they sold many products		
5. I have a cell phone because it is useful		
6. Because companies sell new phones to busy people		
7. Some phones are helpful because they connect to the Internet		
8. Because the invention changed the way people talk to each other		
9. Because they remember what people chose in the past		
10. I do not like this phone because it is too big and too heavy		

2 Match each independent clause (1–8) with a dependent clause (a–h) to make a complete sentence.

1 Some scientists study farms ___ **a** because they can make a lot of money.

2 Many people like chocolate ___ **b** because it helps the environment.

3 Cacao is a familiar crop ___ **c** because they want to help farmers.

4 Some people like natural farming ___ **d** because they learn better ways to farm.

5 Cacao is important ___ **e** because it is sweet.

6 Research helps cacao farmers ___ **f** because many farmers grow it.

7 Small farmers grow cacao ___ **g** because they get better chocolate.

8 Chocolate lovers are happy ___ **h** because it is needed to make chocolate.

CHECK!

1 *Because* is a conjunction. It explains _____. Use *because* to begin a _____ clause.

2 A clause that begins with _____ is a dependent clause. It cannot stand alone. A dependent clause by itself is a sentence _____. You must join a dependent clause with an _____ clause to make a complete sentence.

C. Practice

1 Read the paragraph. How many sentence fragments are there? Check (✓) the correct answer.

¹Thomas Edison is famous because he invented a practical electric lightbulb. ²Because Edison was born in Ohio. ³Lightbulbs helped people because they could do things at night. ⁴Because the day is short. ⁵Before Edison's lightbulb, gas lighting was common. ⁶Because people were used to gas lighting. ⁷Edison's lightbulb was not the first lightbulb, but it was the first practical lightbulb. ⁸Edison did not only invent the lightbulb. ⁹He also invented a system for lighting. ¹⁰Because Edison wanted big changes in the world. ¹¹Now lightbulbs are more efficient. ¹²For example, new lightbulbs save money because they last longer. ¹³Because they help students study later.

☐ a. There are three sentence fragments. Sentences: _____

☐ b. There are four sentence fragments. Sentences: _____

☐ c. There are five sentence fragments. Sentences: _____

2 Read each sentence in the chart. Decide if it has one or two clauses. Check (✓) the box in the correct column.

	ONE CLAUSE	TWO CLAUSES
1. A company wants to sell people tickets to space because they are planning space travel for ordinary people.		
2. The company knows that people like adventure because they realize that many people want to travel to space.		
3. The company is planning to offer space trips by the year 2015.		
4. Some researchers and scientists are trying to learn more about space travel.		
5. There is a close connection between air travel and space travel because they have many things in common.		
6. Scientists are working on solving some problems with space travel because right now, it is expensive and not very comfortable.		
7. Some people like to try a sample before they buy a new product.		
8. The idea of flying far into space is more recent.		
9. The company thinks they will sell a lot of space vacations because many people will pay for the chance to visit somewhere different.		
10. Researchers study the brain because they want to understand it better.		

D. Skill Quiz

Check (✓) the correct answer for each item.

1 *Because* is a conjunction that explains
   - a. what.
   - b. when.
   - c. why.

2 A clause with *because* is
   - a. an independent clause.
   - b. a dependent clause.
   - c. a complete idea.

3 A clause with *because* is a sentence fragment
   - a. when it is by itself.
   - b. when it has an independent clause.
   - c. when it uses another conjunction.

4 The word *because* goes
   - a. at the end of the dependent clause.
   - b. in the middle of the dependent clause.
   - c. at the beginning of the dependent clause.

5 Complete this sentence: *Many people like chocolate ___.*
   - a. they like the taste
   - b. because it is sweet
   - c. they eat it every day

6 Complete this sentence: *Research helps cacao farmers ___.*
   - a. because they learn better ways to farm
   - b. it helps them use natural ways to farm
   - c. they have a new way to farm cacao

7 Complete this sentence: *Hybrid cars are popular ___.*
   - a. they help the environment
   - b. they do not use a lot of gas
   - c. because they save energy

8 Complete this sentence: *New cell phones will be more helpful ___.*
   - a. people will get information from them
   - b. because they will be faster
   - c. why they will know what people like

9 Choose the complete sentence.
   - a. Because people could not work at night.
   - b. Because the light bulb was very important.
   - c. It helped because people could work at night.

10 Choose the sentence fragment.
   - a. He invented it because he wanted to help.
   - b. Because it made travel much easier.
   - c. More people visited their friends.

FAST FOOD OR SLOW FOOD

CONNECTING TO THE THEME

How healthy is your diet?

Which food is the healthiest to eat before a meal?

    A candy   **B** milk and a cookie   **C** carrots

Which food is healthiest to eat after a meal?

    A chocolate cake   **B** crackers and cheese   **C** yogurt

What is the best thing to drink after a meal?

    A soda   **B** orange juice   **C** water

Mostly As: you don't eat very healthily. Mostly Bs: you have a reasonably healthy diet. Mostly Cs: you eat healthily and sensibly.

A. Skill Presentation

An independent clause has a subject and a verb. It expresses a complete idea. A dependent clause has a subject and a verb, but it does not express a complete idea.

A dependent clause begins with a **conjunction**. Conjunctions such as *before* and *after* join an independent clause with a dependent clause. These conjunctions describe **when** something happened.

    Wei ate fast food every day **before** she changed her diet.

Before she changed her diet is the dependent clause. We do not know what happened before she changed her diet when we read only this clause.

    Celia ate fast food **before** she traveled.

The word *before* describes when Celia ate fast food. The dependent clause is *before she traveled*. She ate fast food and then she traveled.

    Josef read the recipe **after** he bought the cookbook.

The word *after* describes when Josef read the recipe. The dependent clause is *after he bought the cookbook*. He bought a cookbook and then he read a recipe.

B. Over to You

1 Read the paragraph. How many sentences have dependent clauses? Check (✓) the correct answer.

¹Brianna changed her diet last year. ²She ate fast food every day before she learned that it had a lot of calories. ³Now she eats healthy food. ⁴She has salads for lunch. ⁵She makes grilled fish for dinner. ⁶She often has a piece of fruit after she eats dinner. ⁷She reads the food information about dishes before she eats at restaurants. ⁸Brianna lost 20 pounds on her diet. ⁹She helped her parents start a new diet after they said they needed to lose weight, too. ¹⁰Brianna and her family are happier and healthier now.

☐ a. There is one sentence with a dependent clause. Sentence: _____
☐ b. There are four sentences with dependent clauses. Sentences: _____
☐ c. There are six sentences with dependent clauses. Sentences: _____

2 Check (✓) the correct clause to complete each sentence.

1 Patricio lost weight after ___.

☐ a. he started his new diet
☐ b. started exercising every day

2 Anabel made healthy dishes after ___.

☐ a. she learned to cook
☐ b. gained weight

3 Cristina ate food with fewer calories after ___.

☐ a. her diet is important to her
☐ b. she took a healthy eating class

4 Miguel started cooking with vegetables after ___.

☐ a. he went on a low-fat diet
☐ b. is much better now

5 Nguyen stopped eating canned foods after ___.

☐ a. he learned they had a lot of sugar
☐ b. started buying natural foods

6 Marcelo did not eat fruit before ___.

☐ a. only ate meat and potato chips
☐ b. he went on a healthy diet

7 Tran was healthier after ___.

☐ a. he stopped eating fast food
☐ b. took a yoga class

8 Pamela reads the ingredients before ___.

☐ a. she eats canned foods
☐ b. she makes salad

9 Meena asked for the recipe after ___.

☐ a. was delicious
☐ b. she tried her grandmother's cake

10 Dana ate fast food before ___.

☐ a. she knew how much salt it had
☐ b. ate healthy foods

CHECK!

1 A _____ clause has a subject and a verb, but it does not express a complete idea.

2 A dependent clause begins with a _____, such as *before* or *after*, which describe _____ something happened.

C. Practice

1 Read each item in the chart. Decide if it is a complete sentence or a sentence fragment. Check (✓) the box in the correct column.

	COMPLETE SENTENCE	SENTENCE FRAGMENT
1. Becky rarely ate fast food		
2. Before she went on a diet		
3. Marianne ate oatmeal for breakfast after she changed her eating habits		
4. Abigail makes food with natural ingredients		
5. After she learned her diet was unhealthy		
6. Jin did not eat canned foods after he learned to cook		
7. Before Anton bought a new cookbook with healthy recipes		
8. Esteban read the food menu before he decided what to eat		
9. Before he orders a dish		
10. Ian ate ice cream sundaes		

2 Check (✓) the sentence in each pair that uses a conjunction to describe when something happened.

1 ☐ a. Manuel lost weight with help from his family.
☐ b. Manuel lost weight after he stopped eating food with a lot of sugar.

2 ☐ a. Marlee counts the calories before she starts cooking.
☐ b. Marlee counts the calories in all the food she eats.

3 ☐ a. Chris washed the vegetables before she cooked them.
☐ b. Chris washed the vegetables and ate them.

4 ☐ a. I love to eat fast food on Friday after I finish work.
☐ b. I love to eat fast food on Fridays.

5 ☐ a. Penny sometimes eats yogurt and honey for dessert.
☐ b. Penny often eats yogurt and honey after a meal.

6 ☐ a. I try to drink a glass of water before I eat a meal.
☐ b. I try to drink a glass of water with every meal.

7 ☐ a. I lost 20 lbs on a diet after starting to eat fish, vegetables, and fruit.
☐ b. I lost 20 lbs on a diet eating fish, vegetables, and fruit.

8 ☐ a. Jenny never read the labels on cans to eat more healthily.
☐ b. Jenny never read the labels on cans before she started to eat more healthily.

D. Skill Quiz

Check (✓) the correct answer for each item.

1 An independent clause has
   - ☐ a. a subject, a verb, and a complete idea.
   - ☐ b. two subjects, two verbs, but no complete idea.
   - ☐ c. a subject, a verb, but no complete idea.

2 A dependent clause has
   - ☐ a. a subject, a verb, and a complete idea.
   - ☐ b. two subjects, two verbs, but no complete idea.
   - ☐ c. a subject, a verb, but no complete idea.

3 An example of a sentence fragment is
   - ☐ a. two independent clauses.
   - ☐ b. a dependent clause with no independent clause.
   - ☐ c. a dependent clause and an independent clause.

4 A dependent clause begins with a conjunction such as
   - ☐ a. *before* or *after*.
   - ☐ b. *and* or *but*.
   - ☐ c. *the* or *a*.

5 Choose the complete sentence.
   - ☐ a. Jeremy knew more about nutrition after he took a class.
   - ☐ b. After he started his diet and stopped eating fast food.
   - ☐ c. Before he took a nutrition class.

6 Choose the complete sentence.
   - ☐ a. After she started eating healthy food every day.
   - ☐ b. Before she started her diet last month.
   - ☐ c. Clara ate better food after she went on a diet.

7 Choose the complete sentence.
   - ☐ a. Mala ate less fast food after she bought a new cookbook.
   - ☐ b. After she bought a new cookbook filled with low-fat recipes.
   - ☐ c. Before she stopped eating fast food every day.

8 Choose the complete sentence.
   - ☐ a. Before my mother bought low-fat desserts at fast food restaurants.
   - ☐ b. My mother gained weight after she ate a lot of desserts at fast food restaurants.
   - ☐ c. After my mother ate fewer low-fat desserts like fruit and frozen yogurt.

9 Choose the complete sentence.
   - ☐ a. I started a diet after I saw my doctor last week.
   - ☐ b. After my appointment at the doctor's office last week.
   - ☐ c. Before I saw my doctor at his office last week.

10 Choose the complete sentence.
   - ☐ a. Daniel has a snack before he eats dinner.
   - ☐ b. Before he eats dinner and dessert.
   - ☐ c. After he has dessert and coffee.

DO WHAT YOU ENJOY DOING

CONNECTING TO THE THEME

How do you prepare to choose your career?

- I develop my interests, and I look for new hobbies.
- I make a list of my favorite classes, but I also think about my least favorite classes.
- I often research new fields, so I know which careers are open to me.
- I try to improve on my weaknesses. I try to get better at things I don't do well.
- I think about where I want to be in five years' time, so I can plan how to get there.

4–5 items: you've given it a lot of thought and done your research. 3 items: you've considered some factors, but not all of them. 1–2 items: you need to do a lot more thinking about what you really want to do.

A. Skill Presentation

A sentence can have one or more independent clauses. Independent clauses are connected with a comma and the conjunctions *and, but,* or *so.*

> Scott played baseball, and he started a sports agency.

A run-on sentence has two or more independent clauses that are combined with no comma or no conjunction. Run-on sentences are grammatically incorrect in English.

> Scott liked baseball he played in college. ✗

There are two ways to avoid run-on sentences. The first way is to make two sentences by adding a **period** after the first independent clause. Begin the second clause with a capital letter.

> Scott liked baseball. He played in college.

The second way to avoid run-on sentences is to add a **conjunction** between the independent clauses. For example, you can add *and, but,* or *so.* Remember to use a **comma**, too.

> Scott liked baseball, **and** he played in college.

B. Over to You

1 Read each item in the chart. Decide if it is correct or if it is a run-on sentence. Check (✓) the box in the correct column.

	CORRECT SENTENCE	RUN-ON SENTENCE
1. I want to be an engineer, but I hate math.		
2. Mr. Larmore loves to travel he became a travel agent.		
3. My brother is a good soccer player, so he wants to play soccer in college.		
4. We like animals, but we do not want a pet.		
5. My father is a successful writer he has written three books.		
6. I enjoy collecting books and I would like to be a librarian.		
7. Frank studied music in college, and he has a job as a drummer.		
8. Jan's hobby is painting she will paint a picture for the art show.		

2 Check (✓) the option that is not a run-on sentence for each item.

1 ☐ a. I love watching movies, so I decided to study acting.
☐ b. I love watching movies so I decided to study acting.
☐ c. I love watching movies I decided to study acting.

2 ☐ a. Sonny likes rules and he is a good police officer.
☐ b. Sonny likes rules, and he is a good police officer.
☐ c. Sonny likes rules he is a good police officer.

3 ☐ a. Michael is good at fixing cars. He is a mechanic.
☐ b. Michael is good at fixing cars he is a mechanic.
☐ c. Michael is good at fixing cars and he is a mechanic.

4 ☐ a. Lee studied law but he did not become a lawyer.
☐ b. Lee studied law he did not become a lawyer.
☐ c. Lee studied law, but he did not become a lawyer.

5 ☐ a. I wanted to work with children I became a teacher.
☐ b. I wanted to work with children. I became a teacher.
☐ c. I wanted to work with children so I became a teacher.

CHECK!

1 A _____ sentence has two or more independent clauses combined with no comma or no _____.

2 Avoid run-on sentences when you write. Make _____ sentences, or use a _____ with a conjunction.

C. Practice

1 Check (✓) the correct answer to fix each run-on sentence.

1 Carrie liked to sing when she was ___ is in the music program now.

☐ a. a child she
☐ b. a child, she
☐ c. a child. She

2 I want to go to ___ work for a good company.

☐ a. college I want to
☐ b. college, and I want to
☐ c. college, I want to

3 My hobbies are painting and ___ working in an art museum is fun.

☐ a. drawing so I think
☐ b. drawing, so I think
☐ c. drawing I think

4 John hates ___ works in a bookstore.

☐ a. reading, but he
☐ b. reading but he
☐ c. reading, he

5 Carson loves ___ will study it more in college.

☐ a. history he
☐ b. history so he
☐ c. history. He

6 Donna wants to be a ___ does not want to work hard.

☐ a. doctor, but she
☐ b. doctor she
☐ c. doctor but she

2 Match each paragraph (A–D) with the correct description (1–4).

___ **1** Correct paragraph

___ **2** Includes run-on sentences

___ **3** Incorrect use of conjunctions

___ **4** Mistakes with commas

A Baseball is Scott Boras's career. He played baseball in college, but after college, he became a professional. Baseball became his job, so later, Boras developed a knee problem. He had to stop playing. However, his interest in baseball did not end. He became a sports agent, but he started a business. It was successful, and his company helps baseball players make more money. Now, Boras works with many famous baseball players. Baseball is his life.

B Baseball is Scott Boras's career. He played baseball in college. After college, he became a professional and baseball became his job. Later, Boras developed a knee problem so he had to stop playing. However, his interest in baseball did not end so he became a sports agent. He started a business. It was successful. His company helps baseball players make more money. Now, Boras works with many famous baseball players. Baseball is his life.

C Baseball is Scott Boras's career. He played baseball in college, and after college, he became a professional. Baseball became his job, but later Boras developed a knee problem. He had to stop playing. However, his interest in baseball did not end. He became a sports agent. He started a business. It was successful. His company helps baseball players make more money, so now Boras works with many famous baseball players. Baseball is his life.

D Baseball is Scott Boras's career he played baseball in college. After college, he became a professional. Baseball became his job. Later, Boras developed a knee problem. He had to stop playing. However, his interest in baseball did not end. He became a sports agent he started a business. It was successful. His company helps baseball players make more money. Now, Boras works with many famous baseball players baseball is his life.

D. Skill Quiz

Check (✓) the correct answer for each item.

1 A run-on sentence has at least
- ☐ a. one independent clause.
- ☐ b. two independent clauses.
- ☐ c. three independent clauses.

2 When you combine two independent clauses, use
- ☐ a. a prepositional phrase.
- ☐ b. a comma and a conjunction.
- ☐ c. a period and a dependent clause.

3 When you write, it is important to
- ☐ a. avoid run-on sentences.
- ☐ b. use many run-on sentences.
- ☐ c. include a lot of long sentences.

4 To fix a run-on sentence, you can
- ☐ a. add another independent clause.
- ☐ b. add a period to make two sentences.
- ☐ c. remove the comma and the conjunction.

5 Choose the run-on sentence.
- ☐ a. I love science, so I am going to be a doctor.
- ☐ b. I love science. I am going to be a doctor.
- ☐ c. I love science so I am going to be a doctor.

6 Choose the run-on sentence.
- ☐ a. Michele loves cooking and she makes us dinner every Friday.
- ☐ b. Michele loves cooking, and she makes us dinner every Friday.
- ☐ c. Michele loves cooking. She makes us dinner every Friday.

7 Choose the run-on sentence.
- ☐ a. Luis likes baseball. His brother does not like sports.
- ☐ b. Luis likes baseball but his brother does not like sports.
- ☐ c. Luis likes baseball, but his brother does not like sports.

8 Choose the answer that fixes this run-on sentence: *My hobby is trying new restaurants I go to a new one every Friday.*
- ☐ a. My hobby is trying new restaurants and I go to a new one every Friday.
- ☐ b. My hobby is trying new restaurants, I go to a new one every Friday.
- ☐ c. My hobby is trying new restaurants. I go to a new one every Friday.

9 Choose the answer that fixes this run-on sentence: *William wants to start a new company he does not have enough money.*
- ☐ a. William wants to start a new company, but he does not have enough money.
- ☐ b. William wants to start a new company, he does not have enough money.
- ☐ c. William wants to start a new company but he does not have enough money.

10 Choose the answer that fixes this run-on sentence: *Darren ran for student council and he won the election.*
- ☐ a. Darren ran for student council, and he won the election.
- ☐ b. Darren ran for student council, he won the election.
- ☐ c. Darren ran for student council so he won the election.

THE YEARS AHEAD

CONNECTING TO THE THEME

How good are your work skills?

Yes **No** I am able to lead a team.

Yes **No** I can work as part of a team and help my colleagues.

Yes **No** I am organized, so I can find information quickly.

Yes **No** I am sociable, but I don't distract others.

Yes **No** I am able to ask for help when I need assistance.

Mostly Yes: you'll do well in the workplace. Mostly No: you should work on some of these skills to improve your chances in the workplace.

A. Skill Presentation

A **simple sentence** has one subject–verb group, and it expresses a complete idea. A simple sentence always has one independent clause.

> Good **employees ask** questions.

> **Vera found** information and wrote reports.

A **compound sentence** has at least two subject–verb groups. It expresses at least two complete ideas. A compound sentence also has at least two independent clauses, which are joined by a **conjunction**. Some conjunctions for compound sentences are *and*, *but*, and *so*. Remember to add a comma before these conjunctions.

> Nina and I have degrees, **but** Stewart has experience.

> Judith learns quickly, **so** she is successful.

A **complex sentence** has at least two subject–verb groups and expresses one complete idea. A complex sentence has an independent clause and a dependent clause. A dependent clause has a subject and a verb, but it does not express a complete idea. A dependent clause always begins with a conjunction. You can use the conjunctions *because*, *if*, and *when* with dependent clauses. Do not write a comma before these conjunctions.

INDEPENDENT CLAUSE	DEPENDENT CLAUSE

> Kim learned computer skills **when** she worked for the phone company.

> You should take that office job **if** you can learn new skills.

B. Over to You

1   Read the letter. How many complex sentences are there? Check (✓) the correct answer.

Dear Ruben,

¹Welcome to the Career Center! ²I am sending this letter because you are going to graduate next month. ³You should meet with one of our job counselors. ⁴They will help you write a resume when you are ready to look for a job. ⁵They will show you online job sites. ⁶They can give you useful information if you are interested in a particular field. ⁷The Career Center has a big computer lab. ⁸You can work on our computers before you meet with your job counselor. ⁹We hope to see you soon.

Good luck,
Dean Shaley

☐   a. There are three complex sentences. Sentences: _____
☐   b. There are four complex sentences. Sentences: _____
☐   c. There are six complex sentences. Sentences: _____

2   Read each sentence in the chart. Decide if it is a simple, compound, or complex sentence. Check (✓) the box in the correct column.

	SIMPLE SENTENCE	COMPOUND SENTENCE	COMPLEX SENTENCE
1. John will get experience when he works in the hospital.			
2. Angelo started a training program, and Sonia is taking classes.			
3. Brianna became a nurse because she likes helping people.			
4. Abdul goes to the career center twice a week.			
5. You will certainly find a job if you keep trying.			
6. Paul and Grace work in the medical field.			
7. Matt needed help with his resume, so he went to the career center			
8. Vivian is polite to her co-workers.			

CHECK!

1 A _____ sentence has one subject–verb group, and it expresses one complete idea.

2 A _____ sentence has at least two independent clauses joined by a _____, such as *and*, *but*, or *so*.

3 A _____ sentence has an independent clause joined to a _____ clause by a conjunction, such as *because*, *if*, or *when*.

C. Practice

1   **Check (✓) the correct answer for each item.**

1   Choose the simple sentence.
- ☐ a. Gabriela is training to become a nurse.
- ☐ b. Gabriela wants to be a nurse, so she studies nursing.
- ☐ c. Gabriela will become a nurse in two years.

2   Choose the compound sentence.
- ☐ a. Neela will study law if she gets into law school.
- ☐ b. Neela is a student, but Pooja is a teacher.
- ☐ c. Pooja and Neela live in the same town.

3   Choose the complex sentence.
- ☐ a. Jeremiah learns new job skills.
- ☐ b. Jeremiah is friendly and polite to his boss.
- ☐ c. Jeremiah is successful because he has good job skills.

4   Choose the simple sentence.
- ☐ a. Marcelo learned to use an e-mail program last year.
- ☐ b. Marcelo is learning to type faster, and Joaquin is helping him.
- ☐ c. Joaquin learned to type fast, so he gets his work done quickly.

5   Choose the compound sentence.
- ☐ a. Steven is learning new skills because he started a new job.
- ☐ b. Steven and Aaron started new jobs at the same company.
- ☐ c. Steven wanted to work in a new field, so he studied marketing.

6   Choose the complex sentence.
- ☐ a. James wants to work for a big company, so he is studying business.
- ☐ b. James will become a businessman when he finishes school.
- ☐ c. James is learning good research skills in school.

2   **Read the paragraph and answer the questions.**

¹Your job can help you learn important work skills, so they will help you in future jobs. ²In almost every job, you need to use computers, and familiarity with common programs like Microsoft Word is extremely valuable. ³Another important skill is finding information you need. ⁴Good employees ask questions, but they are able to learn quickly. ⁵Probably the most important skill is working well with others. ⁶Good employees get along well with their co-workers when they are friendly and polite. ⁷Work on these skills in every job, because you will almost certainly have a more successful career.

1   How many simple sentences does the text have? ___ Sentences: _____

2   How many compound sentences does the text have? ___ Sentences: _____

3   How many complex sentences does the text have? ___ Sentences: _____

4   What conjunctions are used? _____

D. Skill Quiz

Check (✓) the correct answer for each item.

1 An independent clause
- ☐ a. has a subject and a verb but is not a complete idea.
- ☐ b. has two subjects, two verbs, and expresses two complete ideas.
- ☐ c. has a subject and a verb and expresses a complete idea.

2 A dependent clause
- ☐ a. has a subject and a verb but is not a complete idea.
- ☐ b. has two subjects, two verbs, and expresses two complete ideas.
- ☐ c. has a subject and a verb and expresses one complete idea.

3 A simple sentence
- ☐ a. has exactly one independent clause.
- ☐ b. has a dependent clause.
- ☐ c. has two independent clauses.

4 A compound sentence
- ☐ a. has exactly one independent clause.
- ☐ b. has a dependent clause.
- ☐ c. has two independent clauses.

5 A complex sentence
- ☐ a. has two dependent clauses.
- ☐ b. has a dependent clause.
- ☐ c. has two independent clauses.

6 Choose the simple sentence.
- ☐ a. Tran studied engineering, so Anton gave him a job.
- ☐ b. Tran wants to get a new job soon.
- ☐ c. Tran learned new skills when he started his job.

7 Choose the simple sentence.
- ☐ a. Ronaldo gets good grades, but he does not have work experience.
- ☐ b. Ronaldo will get work experience when he graduates.
- ☐ c. Ronaldo joined the engineering program last month.

8 Choose the compound sentence.
- ☐ a. Paolina looked for a new job, and Kara visited the career center.
- ☐ b. Paolina and Kara will visit the career center together.
- ☐ c. Paolina will visit the career center if Kara comes with her.

9 Choose the compound sentence.
- ☐ a. Kyouka works at the hospital because she is a nurse.
- ☐ b. Kyouka lives nearby, so she works at the local hospital.
- ☐ c. Kyouka will work at a different hospital when she moves next month.

10 Choose the complex sentence.
- ☐ a. Amani studied marketing, so she will search for a job in that field.
- ☐ b. Amani will get a job in marketing when she finishes her program.
- ☐ c. Amani hopes to find a job in the marketing field.

WILL WE NEED TEACHERS?

CONNECTING TO THE THEME

What do you think is the future of teaching?

Yes   No   Students in some countries are already being taught by robots. Do you think this could happen in the United States?

Yes   No   Students can watch lectures, presentations, and class discussions online. Do you think this is an effective way to learn?

Yes   No   An article from November 11, 2011 states that 6.2 million students took at least one online class in the fall of 2010. Do you think this number will increase over the next ten years?

Mostly Yes: you believe that teaching will change in the future. Mostly No: you believe that teaching will never change.

A. Skill Presentation

When you write, use the correct punctuation at the end of a sentence. A statement is a sentence that gives information and ends with a period.

I am taking an online course.

A question is a sentence that asks for information. Questions end with a question mark.

Do you like online courses?

Some punctuation goes in the middle of a sentence. With dates, use a comma after the day.

The online lecture is on March fifteenth, two thousand thirteen.

When you write lists with three or more items, use a comma after each item.

Mel studies math, science, and history.

When you write a compound or complex sentence, use a comma. In a compound sentence, use a comma after the first independent clause. (Compound sentences have more than one independent clause, and they use a conjunction like *and*, *but*, or *so*.) In a complex sentence that starts with a dependent clause, use a comma after the dependent clause. (Complex sentences have a dependent clause and an independent clause. The dependent clause can begin with a conjunction like *because*, *before*, or *after*.)

The course is online, so I need a good computer.

After I found the website, I watched a class online.

B. Over to You

1 Read the statements and questions. Add the correct punctuation (period or question mark).

1 Do you like discussing homework online ____

2 Many universities are offering online courses ____

3 Where do you keep your online homework ____

4 How many courses are you taking online ____

5 My first online course started in January ____

6 Robots may replace teachers someday ____

7 Did you return the book ____

8 Our website offers free classes ____

9 Who is your teacher for the online course ____

10 Online courses are a reality ____

2 Read the sentences and add commas where necessary. If no comma is needed, leave it blank.

1 I like to talk about computers robots and other technology.

2 Ken started taking online classes on September 27 2013.

3 I need to replace my old computer but I do not have enough money.

4 Before you go online you should finish your homework.

5 I have classmates in Boston St. Louis and Denver.

6 Kip is taking three online courses so he needs a good computer.

7 We communicate using e-mail text messages and online posts.

8 After you read the assignment you should send the teacher an e-mail.

9 The university wants to offer 100 online courses by January 1 2020.

10 I enrolled in three online courses and I am taking two traditional classes.

CHECK!

1 Use a period to end a _____ that gives information. Use a _____ _____ to end a sentence that asks for information.

2 Use a comma in the middle of sentences to separate _____ and years in dates, as well as items in a _____.

3 Use a _____ in compound and complex sentences. In a compound sentence, put a comma after the first independent clause. In a _____ sentence, put the comma after the dependent clause.

C. Practice

1 Read each sentence in the chart. Decide if the punctuation is correct. Check (✓) the box in the correct column.

	CORRECT PUNCTUATION	INCORRECT PUNCTUATION
1. I am taking four classes.		
2. Who is your favorite teacher?		
3. Are you taking a reading class.		
4. My friend finished school on June 8, 2012.		
5. My favorite class is history?		
6. The new computer lab opens on, October 3 2014.		
7. There are no classes in June, July, and August.		
8. The teacher wants to teach online so I will make sure my computer is ready.		
9. Classes meet Wednesday Thursday and Friday.		
10. I want to send an e-mail message, but I cannot log on to my computer today.		

2 Read the statements and questions. Add the correct punctuation (comma, period, or question mark). If no punctuation is needed, leave it blank.

1 My favorite professor combines classroom teaching and online learning ___ There are some things ___ we learn better in class ___ but there are some things that are easier online ___

2 Does Professor Johnson teach his classes completely online ___ I never see him enter a classroom ___

3 We often discuss the news in our political science class ___ I like talking about current events ___ with other students ___

4 Angela has different folders ___ to keep her assignments for each class ___

5 Do you ever imagine ___ what learning will be like in the future ___

6 I will check my messages ___ when I go online later ___

7 Mindy is taking two classes ___ Her Spanish class is in a classroom ___ but her biology class is online only ___ She uses her sister's computer for the biology class ___

8 Lia borrowed my notes ___ She promised to return them last night ___ but she didn't ___

9 Jason worked hard ___ to make his dream become a reality ___ Now he has everything he wanted ___

10 Whose computer is this ___ It looks really old ___

D. Skill Quiz

Check (✓) the correct answer for each item.

1 A sentence that asks for information ends with a
   - ☐ a. comma.
   - ☐ b. period.
   - ☐ c. question mark.

2 A sentence that gives information ends with a
   - ☐ a. comma.
   - ☐ b. period.
   - ☐ c. question mark.

3 In the middle of sentences, use a
   - ☐ a. comma.
   - ☐ b. period.
   - ☐ c. question mark.

4 Use a comma
   - ☐ a. when you name only one item.
   - ☐ b. in a list of two items.
   - ☐ c. in a list of three or more items.

5 Choose the sentence with the correct punctuation.
   - ☐ a. Michael likes, pizza, hamburgers and chicken.
   - ☐ b. Michael likes pizza, hamburgers, and chicken.
   - ☐ c. Michael likes pizza, hamburgers and, chicken.

6 Choose the sentence with the correct punctuation.
   - ☐ a. Before I met my teacher in person I did not know what she looked like.
   - ☐ b. Before I met my teacher in person, I did not know what she looked like.
   - ☐ c. Before I met my teacher in person, I did not know what she looked like?

7 Choose the sentence with the correct punctuation.
   - ☐ a. Do you want to take reading, writing and literature classes.
   - ☐ b. I want to take reading, writing, and literature classes?
   - ☐ c. When do you want to take reading, writing, and literature classes?

8 Choose the correct punctuation for this sentence: *The classes were at 10:00 a.m. on December 27, 2012 and January 3, 2013* ___
   - ☐ a. ?
   - ☐ b. .
   - ☐ c. ,

9 Choose the correct punctuation for this sentence: *When do you think all courses will be online* ___
   - ☐ a. ,
   - ☐ b. .
   - ☐ c. ?

10 Choose the correct punctuation for this sentence: *I like my teacher, but I have never met him in person* ___
   - ☐ a. ,
   - ☐ b. .
   - ☐ c. ?

Organizing Ideas Before You Write

CONNECTING TO THE THEME

Are you organized when you study?

Before I study, I …

- get everything I need.
- turn off the TV.
- make a to-do list.
- prioritize my tasks, or decide on the most important tasks.
- eat a healthy snack.
- make any necessary phone calls first.
- turn off my cell phone.

4–7 items: you are organized and study effectively.
0–3 items: you could be more organized when you study.

A. Skill Presentation

When you write a paragraph, it is important that your ideas are organized. This helps your reader understand the ideas in the paragraph. Organize your ideas before you write. Start by choosing a main idea. Next, think about ideas that support your main idea. These ideas may give more information or examples about the main idea. To help organize your supporting ideas, write them down. Use words or phrases to list your ideas. Do not write complete sentences.

Next, look at your supporting ideas. Cross out any ideas that do not support your main idea. Here are some ideas for a paragraph about the benefits of a to-do list.

- helps you be organized
- ~~goals are realistic~~   ⟵   The writer crossed these ideas out
- helps you accomplish goals   because they do not give information
- ~~a calendar can also help~~   ⟵   or examples about the main idea.
- helps you concentrate on important tasks

Once you know which ideas you want to include, organize them clearly. There are many ways to organize your ideas. You can organize them by time, space, or importance. The ideas below for a paragraph about making a to-do list are organized by time.

- first, write the to-do list on paper
- next, put it somewhere visible
- then look at your list
- last, check off items on the list

B. Over to You

1 Match each main idea (1–6) with the correct list of supporting ideas (a–f).

___ 1 Studying in a Library

___ 2 Studying at Home

___ 3 Studying with Friends

___ 4 Improving Pronunciation

___ 5 Improving Memorization

___ 6 Improving Test Scores

a regular study schedule, tutor, advice from teacher

b set goals together, don't get distracted, help each other

c concentrate on small pieces of information, repeat small groups of information, group similar ideas together

d practice with a native speaker, listen to English on TV or the radio, practice difficult sounds

e take materials you need, find out the hours, be quiet

f find space away from your family, don't answer the phone, don't stop for personal tasks like washing dishes

2 Read each main idea. Check (✓) the six supporting ideas that go with it.

1 Prioritizing To-do Lists

☐ a. decide which tasks are most important

☐ b. eat a healthy meal before work

☐ c. write down tasks

☐ d. rate items 1, 2, or 3 for importance

☐ e. buy a notebook for the to-do list

☐ f. put 1s first on the to-do list

☐ g. show the to-do list to friends

☐ h. put 2s second on the list

☐ i. put 3s third on the list

2 Taking Notes in Class

☐ a. listen to the teacher carefully

☐ b. don't leave class early

☐ c. don't write down everything

☐ d. write down the most important information

☐ e. make sure your desk is comfortable

☐ f. underline or circle important notes

☐ g. write new words and facts

☐ h. work with a partner when you study

☐ i. write neatly so you can read it later

CHECK!

1 It is important to organize your ideas _____ you write. Choose a main idea, and write down ideas that _____ your main idea.

2 Use words and _____, not sentences, to list ideas. Then _____ any ideas that do not support your main idea.

3 Organize your ideas clearly. Put them in _____ of time, space, or _____.

C. Practice

1   Read each main idea and supporting ideas for a paragraph. Number them in time order.

1 Setting Goals

_____ check off the goals as you finish them

_____ think about goals to reach

_____ cross out the goals that are not realistic

_____ write down all goals

2 Preparing for Exams

_____ study notes, the book, and handouts

_____ take good notes in class

_____ eat a good meal right before an exam

_____ find a quiet place to study

3 Studying with a Friend

_____ then your friend asks you questions

_____ choose a place together

_____ ask your friend questions about the material

_____ meet at the place on time

2   Read the sentences about a to-do list. Number them in the correct order to form a logical paragraph.

A to-do list can help you organize your work.

_____ Check off the tasks when you finish them.

_____ First, write down everything you need to do.

_____ This is called prioritizing.

_____ If you have many different tasks to do, make a list every day.

_____ Keep the list with you, and look at it often.

_____ Prioritizing helps you concentrate on the most important tasks first.

_____ Number your list with the most important tasks first.

A to-do list can help you keep track of your tasks and reach your goals.

D. Skill Quiz

Check (✓) the correct answer for each item.

1 When is the best time to organize your ideas for a paragraph?

☐ a. before you write
☐ b. while you write
☐ c. after you write

2 When organizing your ideas for a paragraph, what do you do first?

☐ a. Choose a conclusion.
☐ b. Choose a main idea.
☐ c. Think about supporting sentences.

3 What is the best way to list ideas for a paragraph?

☐ a. by writing words and phrases
☐ b. by writing complete sentences
☐ c. by writing a complete paragraph

4 On a list of ideas for a paragraph, cross out

☐ a. ideas that explain the main idea.
☐ b. ideas that do not support the main idea.
☐ c. ideas that give examples about the main idea.

5 After you make a list of ideas that support your main idea,

☐ a. write several paragraphs.
☐ b. write a new topic sentence.
☐ c. organize your ideas clearly.

6 Choose the idea that does not support the main idea: *Benefits of To-Do Lists*.

☐ a. help you memorize facts
☐ b. help you reach goals
☐ c. help you be organized

7 Choose the group of ideas that supports the topic: *Being on Time*.

☐ a. ask questions, make eye contact, do not interrupt
☐ b. dress professionally, smile often, shake hands when you meet
☐ c. wear a watch, leave a few minutes early, set an alarm

8 Choose the group of ideas that supports the topic: *Good Time Management*.

☐ a. study rarely, not reaching goals, unrealistic goals
☐ b. make a schedule, make to-do lists, do not waste time
☐ c. comfortable chair, enough light, quiet area

9 For a paragraph about reaching goals, which ideas are organized clearly?

☐ a. check off goals, write the goals down, set goals
☐ b. set goals, write them down, check the goals off
☐ c. write down goals, check the goals off, set goals

10 For a paragraph about memorizing facts, which ideas are organized clearly?

☐ a. write the facts down, read the facts out loud, study them often
☐ b. study facts often, write the facts down, read the facts out loud
☐ c. read the facts out loud, study the facts often, write the facts down

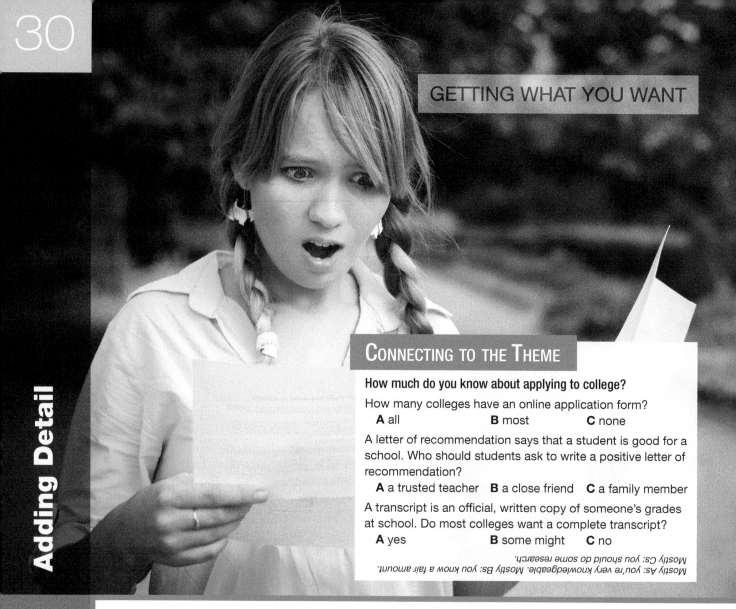

Adding Detail

CONNECTING TO THE THEME

How much do you know about applying to college?

How many colleges have an online application form?

    A all   **B** most   **C** none

A letter of recommendation says that a student is good for a school. Who should students ask to write a positive letter of recommendation?

    A a trusted teacher   **B** a close friend   **C** a family member

A transcript is an official, written copy of someone's grades at school. Do most colleges want a complete transcript?

    A yes   **B** some might   **C** no

Mostly As: you're very knowledgeable. Mostly Bs: you know a fair amount.
Mostly Cs: you should do some research.

A. Skill Presentation

Adding **details** to your writing can make your writing clearer. It can also make your writing more interesting.

> It is easy to open an account.

We can add detail to this sentence to make it clearer.

> It is easy to open a **savings** account.

Adding adjectives gives more detail about the nouns in your sentences.

an account	a banker	a cup of coffee
a **new** account	a **tall** banker	a **hot** cup of coffee

> When I opened an account, a banker gave me a cup of coffee.

> When I opened a **new** account, a **tall** banker gave me a **hot** cup of coffee.

Sentences with adjectives give the reader a clearer and more interesting description.

B. Over to You

1 Read each pair of sentences in the chart. Decide which sentence has more detail and which one has less detail. Check (✓) the box in the correct column.

	MORE DETAIL	LESS DETAIL
1. a. Jennifer is a student in my English class.		
b. Jennifer is a student in my class.		
2. a. There is an old bank on Main Street.		
b. There is a bank on Main Street.		
3. a. I opened an account at a bank.		
b. I opened a checking account at a bank.		
4. a. I have a big deadline on Friday.		
b. I have a deadline on Friday.		

2 Check (✓) the paragraph in each pair that has more detail.

1 ☐ **A**   John applied to a small college in May. He researched several colleges online first. He filled out a long application for one college. Then he asked his English teacher to write a letter of recommendation. He sent his official transcript to the college. He asked for help with applying for student loans. There were some difficult sections, but he completed them on time.

    ☐ **B**   John applied to college in May. He researched colleges online first. He filled out an application for one college. Then he asked a teacher to write a letter of recommendation. He sent his transcript to the college. He asked for information about loans. John had questions while he worked on the application, but he completed it on time.

2 ☐ **A**   Lorena wants to buy a car. She went to a bank. She talked to a banker about an auto loan. The banker said she could apply. She filled out the application and was approved. She hopes to buy a car next week.

    ☐ **B**   Lorena wants to buy a new car. She went to a large bank. She talked to a knowledgeable banker about an auto loan. The banker said she could apply for a large loan. She filled out the application and was approved. She hopes to buy a car next week.

CHECK!

1 Adding details can make your writing _____. It can also make your writing more _____.

2 Using _____ is one way to add details about the _____ in your sentences.

C. Practice

1 **Check (✓) the two words that add detail in each sentence.**

1 The official deadline for the large scholarship is May 12.

- ☐ a. official, scholarship
- ☐ b. official, large
- ☐ c. deadline, May

2 Jenny filled out the long application with a black pen.

- ☐ a. Jenny, pen
- ☐ b. filled, application
- ☐ c. long, black

3 The organization made hot coffee for the informational meeting.

- ☐ a. made, meeting
- ☐ b. hot, informational
- ☐ c. organization, coffee

4 The short keywords helped me with my difficult search.

- ☐ a. short, difficult
- ☐ b. the, my
- ☐ c. keywords, search

5 Marcos might get a huge scholarship and a small loan.

- ☐ a. Marcos, loan
- ☐ b. might, get
- ☐ c. huge, small

6 Tim sent his outstanding transcript to his helpful counselor.

- ☐ a. transcript, counselor
- ☐ b. Tim, sent
- ☐ c. outstanding, helpful

7 They served black coffee at the international conference.

- ☐ a. served, coffee
- ☐ b. They, conference
- ☐ c. black, international

8 We opened a new account with a global bank.

- ☐ a. new, global
- ☐ b. opened, with
- ☐ c. We, account

9 Daniela ate cold pizza with spicy cheese for lunch.

- ☐ a. cold, spicy
- ☐ b. pizza, cheese
- ☐ c. with, for

10 The knowledgeable banker helped me open a new account.

- ☐ a. helped, open
- ☐ b. knowledgeable, new
- ☐ c. banker, account

2 **Circle one word in each sentence that adds detail.**

1 Marcos applied to an impressive college.

2 He completed a detailed application.

3 His teachers wrote positive letters of recommendation.

4 Marcos sent a complete transcript of his grades.

5 He was an excellent student.

6 He hopes for a large scholarship.

7 He visited the financial aid office to learn about tuition fees.

8 Marcos got helpful advice from an adviser.

9 He made a careful plan for his money.

10 Marcos plans to be an active student on campus.

D. Skill Quiz

Check (✓) the correct answer for each item.

1 What is one way to make your writing more interesting?
- ☐ a. Use a subject.
- ☐ b. Add details.
- ☐ c. Include a verb.

2 What is one benefit of adding details to your writing?
- ☐ a. It can make your ideas clearer.
- ☐ b. It can help you think of new ideas.
- ☐ c. It helps you organize your ideas.

3 To add details to nouns, use
- ☐ a. adjectives.
- ☐ b. conjunctions.
- ☐ c. verbs.

4 Choose the adjective that adds detail in this sentence: *The banker gave me a hot cup of coffee.*
- ☐ a. coffee
- ☐ b. banker
- ☐ c. hot

5 Choose the adjective that adds detail in this sentence: *The helpful banker opened my account.*
- ☐ a. helpful
- ☐ b. banker
- ☐ c. account

6 Choose the adjectives that add detail in this sentence: *The difficult application for an important scholarship is due on Monday.*
- ☐ a. application, scholarship
- ☐ b. difficult, important
- ☐ c. due, Monday

7 Choose the sentence that uses an adjective to add detail.
- ☐ a. Jake completed the long application yesterday.
- ☐ b. Jake completed the application.
- ☐ c. Jake completed the application at 9:00 a.m.

8 Choose the sentence that uses an adjective to add detail.
- ☐ a. The bank keeps money in a room in the back.
- ☐ b. The bank keeps money in a room called a vault.
- ☐ c. The bank keeps money in a special room.

9 Choose the sentence that uses an adjective to add detail.
- ☐ a. Jill is spending her money on a good education.
- ☐ b. Jill is spending her money on education.
- ☐ c. Jill is spending her money on an education at State College.

10 Choose the sentence that uses an adjective to add detail.
- ☐ a. Don opened an account on Tuesday.
- ☐ b. Don opened a new account on Tuesday.
- ☐ c. Don and Sarah opened an account on Tuesday.

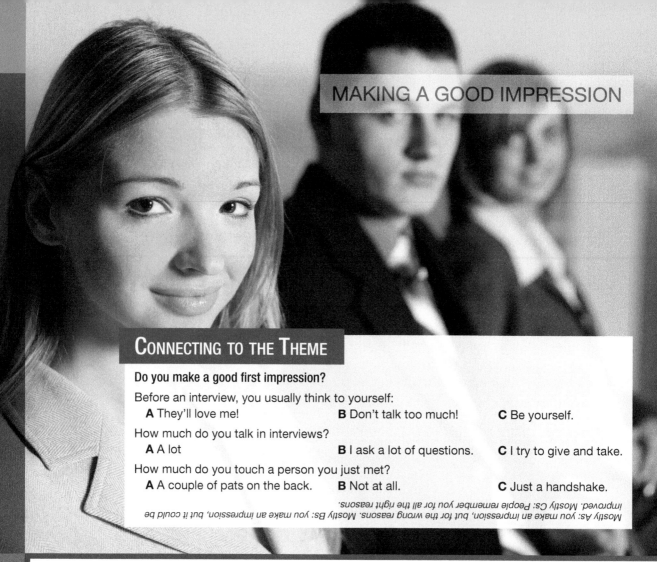

Sentence Order in Paragraphs

MAKING A GOOD IMPRESSION

CONNECTING TO THE THEME

Do you make a good first impression?

Before an interview, you usually think to yourself:

    A They'll love me!   **B** Don't talk too much!   **C** Be yourself.

How much do you talk in interviews?

    A A lot   **B** I ask a lot of questions.   **C** I try to give and take.

How much do you touch a person you just met?

    A A couple of pats on the back.   **B** Not at all.   **C** Just a handshake.

Mostly As: you make an impression, but for the wrong reasons. Mostly Bs: you make an impression, but it could be improved. Mostly Cs: People remember you for all the right reasons.

A. Skill Presentation

When you write paragraphs, put the sentences in the correct order. Start with a topic sentence. Next, write supporting sentences that relate to your main idea. End with a concluding sentence.

It is also important for your supporting sentences to be in a clear order. Put sentences with related ideas near each other. This helps your reader understand your ideas.

Look at the examples of supporting sentences below. In the first example, the related ideas about materials are not together. In the second example, the ideas about being calm are next to each other, and the ideas about materials are next to each other. This will make the ideas in the finished paragraph clearer.

> Make sure you have all the materials you need. It is important to be calm when you speak in front of people. Speak slowly and try not to be too nervous. Remember to bring your notes, handouts, and a bottle of water. ✗

> It is important to be calm when you speak in front of people. Speak slowly and try not to be too nervous. Make sure you have all the materials you need. Remember to bring your notes, any handouts, and a bottle of water. ✓

B. Over to You

1 Read each item in the chart. Decide if the sentences are related or not related to each other. Check (✓) the box in the correct column.

	RELATED	NOT RELATED
1. It is important to dress well for work. For example, wear a suit or a nice top and pants.		
2. Wear a good suit for interviews. It is important to practice with friends.		
3. You can impress your boss with what you wear. A professional suit makes a good first impression.		
4. Before you start an interview, shake hands firmly. Eye contact is important during a presentation.		
5. Be careful if you wear jewelry during a presentation. Dirty hair makes a bad impression.		
6. Wear comfortable shoes if you give a speech. You might have to stand for a long time.		
7. Don't wear a hat when you give a speech. Some people think it is impolite.		
8. After you finish your speech, you can relax. You might be nervous for your first interview.		

2 Read the sentences about casual Fridays. Number them in the correct order so the related ideas are next to each other.

Paul's office has casual Fridays.

___ For example, baseball caps are not allowed.

___ Everyone in Paul's office wears casual clothes on Fridays.

___ However, employees cannot wear hats.

___ Many people wear sneakers.

___ The employees can wear casual shirts and pants.

___ Most people wear T-shirts and jeans.

___ They are also allowed to wear more comfortable shoes.

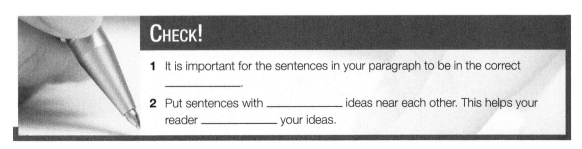

CHECK!

1 It is important for the sentences in your paragraph to be in the correct

_____.

2 Put sentences with _____ ideas near each other. This helps your

reader _____ your ideas.

C. Practice

1 **Check (✓) the paragraph in each pair where the bold sentence is next to a related sentence.**

1 ☐ **A** Many companies allow "business casual" clothes. This means employees do not have to wear dress clothes every day. **The clothes should be neat and clean.** They do not wear suits five days a week. One example of a business casual outfit for women is a sweater and comfortable pants. Business casual makes working comfortable. Remember that there are still appropriate ways to dress.

☐ **B** Many companies allow "business casual" clothes. This means employees do not have to wear dress clothes every day. They do not wear suits five days a week. One example of a business casual outfit for women is a sweater and comfortable pants. **The sweater and pants should be neat and clean.** Business casual makes working comfortable. Remember that there are still appropriate ways to dress.

2 ☐ **A** When you give a speech, look at your audience. It is important to smile during your speech. **Smiling lets your audience know you enjoy what you are talking about.** Speak in a clear voice so your audience can understand you. Speaking slowly will also help them understand what you are saying, and you will seem confident. If you seem confident, you will probably give a better speech.

☐ **B** When you give a speech, look at your audience. It is important to smile during your speech. Speak in a clear voice so your audience can understand you. Speaking slowly will also help them understand what you are saying, and you will seem confident. **Smiling lets your audience know you enjoy what you are talking about.** If you seem confident, you will probably give a better speech.

2 **Read the paragraph and insert the sentences (a–h) in the correct places.**

Do you know the expression, "Practice makes perfect?" It's true! [1]___ If you have to give a presentation at school or work, ask your friends or co-workers to listen to it first. They can give you useful feedback about your presentation. [2]___ Ask your friends for advice about what to change. [3]___ Make sure you have everything you need. [4]___ It is important to be calm when you speak in front of people. Take a few deep breaths before you start a presentation. [5]___ Speak clearly, and don't speak too softly. [6]___ People will listen if you sound as if know what you are talking about. [7]___ By following these tips, your presentation will be successful. [8]___

a Try to appear confident.
b They can tell you what you did well and what you could do better.
c For example, if you have notes to refer to, you will feel more comfortable.
d You may even get an A!
e Doing something many times helps you do it better.
f You want your audience to understand what you are saying.
g They might be able to share some good ideas.
h That will help you if you feel nervous.

D. Skill Quiz

Check (✓) the correct answer for each item.

1 What is the correct order for sentences in a paragraph?

  ☐ a. topic sentence, concluding sentence, supporting sentences

  ☐ b. concluding sentence, supporting sentences, topic sentence

  ☐ c. topic sentence, supporting sentences, concluding sentence

2 What is a good way to put supporting sentences in a clear order?

  ☐ a. Put words in alphabetical order.

  ☐ b. Put related ideas together.

  ☐ c. Put unrelated ideas together.

3 Putting related sentences together

  ☐ a. helps make your ideas clear.

  ☐ b. may confuse your reader.

  ☐ c. gives a conclusion.

4 *You cannot wear jeans or shorts to work.*
  Which sentence is related to this sentence?

  ☐ a. You should wear a suit for an interview.

  ☐ b. You cannot wear hats either.

  ☐ c. It is important to have a nice haircut.

5 *It is important to be confident at work.*
  Which sentence is related to this sentence?

  ☐ a. For example, try not to be nervous when you speak during meetings.

  ☐ b. It is a good idea to wear a dark suit.

  ☐ c. You should make eye contact with your teacher.

6 *First impressions are important.*
  Which sentence is related to this sentence?

  ☐ a. An organized office helps you stay organized.

  ☐ b. Bonnie's office has casual Fridays.

  ☐ c. It is always good to dress neatly.

7 *Keep your work area neat and clean.*
  Which sentence is related to this sentence?

  ☐ a. A neat hairstyle makes a good impression.

  ☐ b. A messy office can make a bad impression.

  ☐ c. It takes practice to give a good speech.

8 *Stand up straight when you give a presentation.*
  Which sentence is related to this sentence?

  ☐ a. Your chair should be near your desk.

  ☐ b. It makes you look confident.

  ☐ c. Speak with a clear voice on the phone.

9 Choose the sentences that are in a clear order.

  ☐ a. Your bag makes an impression during an interview. Your briefcase or purse should be clean. Your shoes should also be clean.

  ☐ b. Your bag makes an impression during an interview. Your shoes should also be clean. Your briefcase or purse should be clean.

10 Choose the sentences that are in a clear order.

  ☐ a. Speak slowly during your speech. You need to speak clearly, too. Make eye contact with your audience. If you look at people, they will think you are confident.

  ☐ b. You need to speak clearly, too. If you look at people, they will think you are confident. Speak slowly during your speech. Make eye contact with your audience.

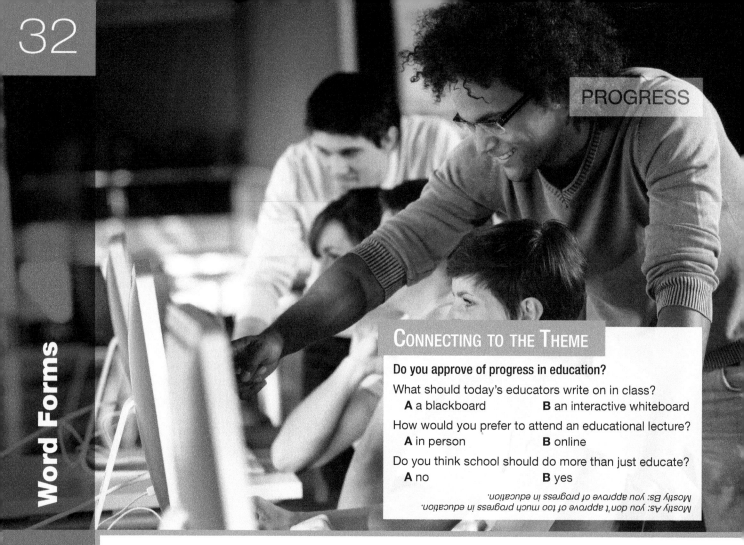

Word Forms

Do you approve of progress in education?

What should today's educators write on in class?
  A a blackboard   **B** an interactive whiteboard

How would you prefer to attend an educational lecture?
  A in person   **B** online

Do you think school should do more than just educate?
  A no   **B** yes

Mostly As: you don't approve of too much progress in education.
Mostly Bs: you approve of progress in education.

A. Skill Presentation

Words that are closely related but are different parts of speech are called **word forms**. Some nouns, verbs, and adjectives express related ideas, but each word is a different part of speech.

Nouns can be the names of people, places, things, or ideas. **Verbs** can express an action. They can also express a quality a person has, or show that a noun belongs to someone. **Adjectives** describe, or give details about, a noun.

> The **creation** of the television changed the world.
>
> Inventors **created** ways of watching TV on cell phones.
>
> John has a **creative** idea for a TV show.

In a sentence, the other words help you know what part of speech a word is. In the first sentence, the word *The* helps us know that *creation* is a noun. In the second sentence, the word *created* comes after the noun *Inventors*, so we know it is a verb. In the third sentence, the word *creative* comes before the noun *idea*, so we know it is an adjective.

Not all words have related forms, but many words do. You can use a dictionary for help with different word forms.

B. Over to You

1 **Look at the bold word in each sentence. Match the sentences (1–6) with the related word forms (a–f).**

___ 1 A skill like **creativity** can help you make progress.

___ 2 They encourage their staff in the **development** of new skills.

___ 3 New technology helps teachers **instruct** their students.

___ 4 Some **memorable** changes happened in the twentieth century.

___ 5 Many corporations **succeed** because they have good leaders.

___ 6 The photograph was a **symbolic** image of our changing world.

a success, successful

b instructor, instructional

c symbol, symbolize

d develop, developmental

e memory, memorize

f creation, create

2 **Read each sentence in the chart. Decide if the word in bold is a noun, verb, or adjective. Check (✓) the box in the correct column.**

	NOUN	VERB	ADJECTIVE
1. **Organization** is important in this class.			
2. Ms. Simms teaches **organizational** skills to her students.			
3. Paula **organizes** her time well.			
4. The **development** of television started more than 75 years ago.			
5. John **developed** a new idea for his company.			
6. Madison works for a **developmental** research company.			
7. Mia **succeeded** in meeting her goals.			
8. The TV show *Friends* was a **success** for many years.			

CHECK!

1 Some nouns, verbs, and adjectives are _____ to each other.

2 It is important to use the _____ form of a word when you write to help make your ideas _____.

3 Use a _____ for help with word forms.

C. Practice

1 Choose the correct form of the word to complete each sentence. Write *N*, *V*, or *Adj*.

___ **1** Who is your *instruct (V) instructor (N) instructional (Adj)* for the film class?

___ **2** I like to *memory (N) memorable (Adj) memorize (V)* lines from TV programs.

___ **3** That *symbol (N) symbolize (V) symbolic (Adj)* has a special meaning.

___ **4** Every year, we *organizational (Adj) organization (N) organize (V)* our work files.

___ **5** Jake is a *creation (N) creative (Adj) create (V)* designer.

___ **6** Our team *develops (V) development (N) developmental (Adj)* ideas together.

___ **7** My instructor is very *succeed (V) success (N) successful (Adj)*. Nearly 100 percent of his students graduate each year.

___ **8** Smartboards provide *entertainment (N) entertaining (Adj) entertain (V)* for young children as well as being educational.

___ **9** They *creation (N) created (V) creative (Adj)* new ways to watch shows on cell phones at that company.

___ **10** My *memorize (V) memorable (Adj) memory (N)* is not as good as it was in the past.

2 Complete each sentence with the correct form of the word in parentheses.

1 What do you know about the twentieth century? Do you think life was more _____ in the 1900s? (create)

2 Everyone has a different opinion about whether life was better years ago. Some people think it was _____ and a time of great achievement. (memory)

3 Many people say that life is more _____ now. They think there is more to do than there was in the past. (entertain)

4 Technology has _____ a lot. For example, computers are faster and smaller. (develop)

5 _____ has improved in the past 30 years. People can e-mail others anywhere in the world. A lot of people also keep in touch using cell phones. (communicate)

6 Some people say that life is more _____ now. They think things are easier than they were in the past. (organize)

7 Some people say our world is too _____. There are too many choices, and it is difficult to make decisions. (complicate)

8 It can be hard for a small family business to _____. However, many big corporations are very successful. (success)

9 Some people feel this _____ big changes, but others think it has been happening slowly over time. (symbol)

10 Many people say life is more _____ today. It is impossible to know for sure. (agree)

D. Skill Quiz

Check (✓) the correct answer for each item.

1 Word forms are nouns, verbs, and adjectives that
- ☐ a. people usually avoid.
- ☐ b. are related.
- ☐ c. must be capitalized.

2 Use correct word forms to help make your ideas
- ☐ a. shorter.
- ☐ b. clearer.
- ☐ c. more important.

3 You can use ___ to help you with word forms.
- ☐ a. a TV
- ☐ b. a pencil
- ☐ c. a dictionary

4 ___, *memorize, memorable*
Which noun is related to these words?
- ☐ a. memory
- ☐ b. musician
- ☐ c. meeting

5 *symbol,* ___, *symbolic*
Which verb is related to these words?
- ☐ a. organize
- ☐ b. simplify
- ☐ c. symbolize

6 *creation, create,* ___
Which adjective is related to these words?
- ☐ a. curious
- ☐ b. creative
- ☐ c. creamy

7 Choose the correct word form to complete this sentence: *The ___ will be built in eight months.*
- ☐ a. development
- ☐ b. develop
- ☐ c. developmental

8 Choose the correct word form to complete this sentence: *The TV station will ___ its network to more countries.*
- ☐ a. expansion
- ☐ b. expand
- ☐ c. expandable

9 Choose the correct word form to complete this sentence: *How many ___ do you belong to?*
- ☐ a. organizations
- ☐ b. organizes
- ☐ c. organizational

10 Choose the correct word form to complete this sentence: *Our teacher asked us to watch an ___ show on TV.*
- ☐ a. instruction
- ☐ b. instruct
- ☐ c. instructional

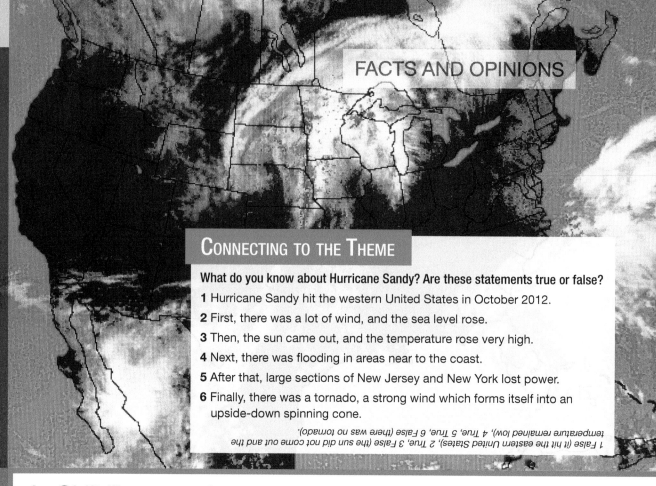

FACTS AND OPINIONS

CONNECTING TO THE THEME

What do you know about Hurricane Sandy? Are these statements true or false?

1 Hurricane Sandy hit the western United States in October 2012.

2 First, there was a lot of wind, and the sea level rose.

3 Then, the sun came out, and the temperature rose very high.

4 Next, there was flooding in areas near to the coast.

5 After that, large sections of New Jersey and New York lost power.

6 Finally, there was a tornado, a strong wind which forms itself into an upside-down spinning cone.

1 False (it hit the eastern United States), 2 True, 3 False (the sun did not come out and the temperature remained low), 4 True, 5 True, 6 False (there was no tornado).

A. Skill Presentation

When you write a paragraph, it is important to organize your ideas. One way to organize ideas is by **time**. When you organize your ideas by time, put them in the order that they happen, and use the **time words** *first, second, third*, as well as *next, after that, later,* and *finally*. These words make your ideas easier for your reader to follow.

> The southern United States experienced three big storms last February. **First**, a blizzard happened on February 5. A blizzard is a big snowstorm with a lot of wind. There was a lot of snow in Virginia and Washington, D.C. It was very dangerous. **Second**, a snowstorm happened on February 9. Some places in Maryland had a lot of snow. **Third**, another snowstorm happened on February 25. **After that**, the snow melted. It also rained a lot. **Later**, there were floods.

You can also use phrases with prepositions to show time order in your writing. The prepositions *in*, *at*, and *on* can be used with nouns related to time. Some nouns related to time are words for seasons, years, months, times, days, and dates.

| in the spring | in 2010 | in January | at 6:00 | on Saturday | on October 10 |

The paragraph below about natural disasters in the United States is organized by the seasons in which the events happen, and it uses phrases with prepositions to help show time order.

> Tornado season is in the spring. Tornadoes usually happen in central states. States with a hot climate can have dangerous heat waves in the summer. This often happens in southern states. Hurricane season is in the fall. Places with a cold climate have blizzards in the winter. They can be very dangerous.

B. Over to You

1 **Match each sentence (1–8) with an event that happened later (a–h). Use the time order words and phrases with prepositions to help you.**

1 First, check a tourism website for the city you want to visit.

2 Next, find out which area you want to stay in.

3 Tokyo is hot in the summer.

4 The population of Tokyo was about 12 million in 2000.

5 The tour of the historic area is on Tuesday.

6 There is an important meeting on January 15.

7 Kolkata became the capital of India in 1772.

8 The warning for the storm was announced at 9:15 a.m.

___ **a** It is sometimes hot in the fall, too.

___ **b** New Delhi became the capital in 1911.

___ **c** The mayor will talk about the meeting on TV on January 18.

___ **d** After that, make a hotel reservation in that city.

___ **e** Second, check the weather on the website.

___ **f** The storm came at 11:00 a.m. on the same day.

___ **g** The tour of the local museums is on Wednesday.

___ **h** It was about 13 million in 2010.

2 **Read the topic sentences. Number the remaining sentences in the correct time order to make logical paragraphs.**

1 There is an important town meeting on October 15.

___ Lunch will be at 12:00 p.m.

___ The meeting will start at 9:00 a.m.

___ Mr. Johnson will talk about the new library at 11:00 a.m.

___ At 9:30, the mayor will talk about safety during hurricanes.

2 There have been many historic blizzards in the United States.

___ During the Knickerbocker Storm in 1922, a theater fell.

___ More than 100 people died because of a blizzard in 1996.

___ People had to sleep in schools during a blizzard in 1977.

___ In 1857, there were over two feet of snow during the Cold Storm.

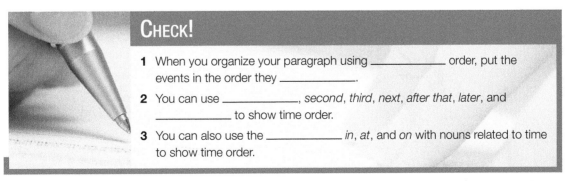

CHECK!

1 When you organize your paragraph using _____ order, put the events in the order they _____.

2 You can use _____, *second*, *third*, *next*, *after that*, *later*, and _____ to show time order.

3 You can also use the _____ *in*, *at*, and *on* with nouns related to time to show time order.

C. Practice

1 **Complete the sentences using the correct verb or time order words.**

listen   finally   first   use
third   do   second   after that

> **Hurricane Safety**
>
> There are many things you can do during a hurricane to be safe. _____, listen to the radio for information. _____ a radio with batteries. _____, turn off the electricity. This will protect your computer and TV. _____, go to a safe place in your house. _____ not sit or stand by windows. _____, lie down on the floor when the hurricane comes. _____, continue to listen to the radio. _____ for instructions on the news if you need to leave your house.

2 **Number the sentences in each item in the correct order to make logical paragraphs.**

1

____ An earthquake in 1957 caused a tsunami in Alaska.

____ There was also a historic earthquake in Alaska in 1964.

____ An earthquake killed 3,000 people in California in 1906.

2

____ Finally, move to a higher floor or the roof, and call for help.

____ Next, move important things to a higher floor, if possible.

____ Second, turn off the electricity.

____ First, bring in things that are outside.

3

In February 2010, three blizzards hit the eastern United States.

____ Then, on February 25, a third blizzard started.

____ The first blizzard started on February 5, 2010.

____ A second blizzard started on February 9.

____ A blizzard is a big storm.

____ In the central part of this first blizzard, there were over 36 inches of snow.

____ Over 20 inches of snow fell.

____ It also dropped more than 20 inches in some places.

____ They happen when it is very cold.

The blizzards of 2010 were historic because they came one right after the other.

D. Skill Quiz

Check (✓) the correct answer for each item.

1 When you organize ideas by time, what order are they in?

☐ a. the order that things appear
☐ b. the order of importance
☐ c. the order the events happen

2 Which words are in the correct time order?

☐ a. first, finally, after that, second
☐ b. first, second, after that, finally
☐ c. finally, first, second, after that

3 Which type of word can follow a preposition to show time order?

☐ a. a verb
☐ b. a noun
☐ c. an adjective

4 Which phrases show time order?

☐ a. in 1995, in April, in the spring
☐ b. in Chicago, in Illinois, in the United States
☐ c. in class, at home, on time

5 Choose the time word that completes this sentence: ___, *shut all the windows. Second, go to a safe place.*

☐ a. Finally
☐ b. Next
☐ c. First

6 Choose the time word that completes this sentence: *Next, call for help. ___, wait until help arrives.*

☐ a. Finally
☐ b. Second
☐ c. First

7 Choose the time word or time phrase that completes this sentence: *Third, put warm clothing on. ___, you can go outside in the snow.*

☐ a. Second
☐ b. After that
☐ c. First

8 Choose the time phrase that completes this sentence: *The blizzard started ___.*

☐ a. at 5:00 p.m.
☐ b. in Boston
☐ c. on the coast

9 Choose the time phrase that completes this sentence: *The population of this city grew quickly ___.*

☐ a. in my house
☐ b. in the 1990s
☐ c. in this city

10 Choose the time phrase that completes this sentence: *The meeting was on February 12, and there was an article about the meeting in the paper ___.*

☐ a. on February 1
☐ b. on February 8
☐ c. on February 13

action verb: a verb such as *eat*, *celebrate*, or *give* that describes an action; it tells what a noun is doing (See Skill 5.)

adjective: a word that describes a noun; for example, *hungry*, *sweet*, or *good* (See Skill 19.)

capital letter: the form of a letter used to begin sentences and proper nouns; it is usually bigger than a lowercase letter (See Skill 1.)

capitalize: to make the first letter of a word a capital letter (See Skill 3.)

clause (also called a *subject–verb group*): a group of words that has a subject and a verb (See Skill 23.)

comma: a punctuation mark (,) used between words and numbers in a sentence; for example, *January 1, 2013* (See Skill 2.)

complex sentence: a sentence with an independent clause and a dependent clause joined by a conjunction such as *because*, *if*, or *when* (See Skill 23.)

compound sentence: a sentence that has at least two independent clauses; it expresses at least two complete ideas (See Skill 15.)

concluding sentence: a sentence that repeats the main idea of a paragraph; it is usually the last sentence in a paragraph (See Skill 14.)

conjunction: a word such as *and*, *but*, *because*, or *if* that joins single words or groups of words (See Skill 15.)

dependent clause: a clause that has a subject and a verb but does not express a complete idea; it cannot be used alone as a complete sentence (See Skill 23.)

detail: a specific fact or piece of information (See Skill 30.)

example: something that illustrates a rule (See Skill 29.)

formatting: the way a piece of writing looks; paragraph formatting includes indentation and space between sentences (See Skill 11.)

indent: to add space before the first word in a paragraph (See Skill 1.)

independent clause: a group of words that has a subject and a verb and expresses a complete idea; it can be used alone as a complete sentence (See Skill 23.)

irregular plural noun: a plural noun that does not end in *–s*; for example, *women* or *people* (See Skill 4.)

irrelevant sentence: a sentence that does not relate to the main idea of a paragraph (See Skill 22.)

letter: a symbol such as *a*, *b*, *c*, or *d* used to write words (See Skill 1.)

list: words or phrases that are arranged one below the other (See Skill 29.)

lowercase letter: the small form of a letter; it is usually smaller than a capital letter (See Skill 3.)

main idea: what a paragraph is about (See Skill 12.)

main verb: a verb used alone in a sentence or with an auxiliary verb (See Skill 10.)

non-action verb (also called a *stative verb*): a verb such as *be*, *have*, or *like* that describes a quality or shows that something belongs to someone; it does not describe an action (See Skill 5.)

noun: a word that names a person, place, thing, or idea; for example, *sister*, *Bangkok*, or *folder* (See Skill 4.)

object: a noun that answers the question *What?* or *Who?* about the verb in a sentence; it comes after the verb in a statement (See Skill 8.)

organize: to put things in a special order (See Skill 29.)

paragraph: a group of sentences about one topic; it has special formatting (See Skill 1.)

part of speech: a category that tells how a word is used in a sentence; for example, *noun*, *adjective*, or *verb* (See Skill 32.)

period: a punctuation mark (.) used to show where the end of a statement is (See Skill 1.)

phrase: a group of words (See Skill 29.)

plural noun: a noun that refers to more than one person, place, thing, or idea; for example, *women* or *letters* (See Skill 4.)

preposition: a word that helps show location or time; for example, *in*, *on*, or *at* (See Skill 10.)

prepositional phrase: a preposition followed by a noun; for example, *at noon*, *in Boston*, or *on Monday* (See Skill 10.)

pronoun: a word used in place of a noun; for example, *you* or *we* (See Skill 3.)

proper noun: the name of a specific person, place, or thing; it is capitalized (See Skill 7.)

punctuation marks: special marks used in writing such as a period (.), a question mark (?), or a comma (,) (See Skill 2.)

question: a sentence that asks for information; it ends with a question mark (?) (See Skill 2.)

question mark: a punctuation mark (?) used at the end of a sentence to show that it is a question (See Skill 2.)

question word: a word that is often the first word in a question; for example, *who, what, where, when, why,* or *how* (See Skill 2.)

regular plural noun: a plural noun that ends in *–s*; for example, *sisters* or *meetings* (See Skill 4.)

run-on sentence: two or more independent clauses connected without a comma or a conjunction (See Skill 26.)

sentence: a group of words that has a subject and a verb and expresses a complete idea (See Skill 6.)

sentence fragment: a group of words that does not express a complete idea (See Skill 9.)

sentence order: the way sentences are arranged in a paragraph (See Skill 31.)

simple sentence: a sentence that has one subject-verb group; it expresses one complete idea (See Skill 15.)

singular noun: a noun that refers to one person, place, thing, or idea; for example, *woman* or *office* (See Skill 4.)

statement: a sentence that gives information; it ends with a period (.) (See Skill 2.)

subject: the person, place, or thing that does the action in a sentence (See Skill 6.)

subject–verb group (also called a *clause*): a group of words that has a subject and a verb (See Skill 15.)

supporting sentence: a sentence in a paragraph that gives more information about the topic sentence; it is directly related to the main idea (See Skill 13.)

time order: the order that events happen (See Skill 33.)

time word: a word that shows time order; for example, *first, second, third,* or *next* (See Skill 33.)

title: an introduction to a name; for example, *Mr., Ms.,* or *Dr.* (See Skill 7.)

topic: what a piece of writing is about (See Skill 12.)

topic sentence: a sentence that tells the main idea of a paragraph; it is often the first sentence in a paragraph (See Skill 12.)

verb: a word that describes an action or a state; it tells what someone or something is doing or being (See Skill 5.)

word: a group of letters that has meaning (See Skill 1.)

word forms: words that are closely related but are different parts of speech; for example, *creation, create,* and *creative* (See Skill 32.)

word order: the way words are placed in a sentence; in English, the correct order for a statement is subject, then verb, then object (See Skill 8.)

What are the most common words in academic English? Which words appear most frequently in readings in different academic subject areas? Dr. Averil Coxhead, who is currently a Senior Lecturer at Victoria University of Wellington in New Zealand, did research to try to answer this question. The result was the Academic Word List (AWL), a list of 570 words or word families that appear in academic readings in many different academic fields. These words are extremely useful for students to know. In *Skills for Effective Writing*, you will encounter a number of these words in context.

The following is a list of the AWL words in *Skills for Effective Writing 1* and the Skills where they appear.

academic	12; 14; 22	commitment	14
achieve	12; 14	communicate	21; 28; 32
achievement	32	communication	21–23
administrative	5	community	14
adult	14; 17	complex	23; 27–28
affect	16; 22	compound	15; 17; 20; 27–28
aid	22; 30	computer	2–3; 14; 20–21; 24; 27–28; 32–33
appropriate	31	concentrate	16; 29
area	12; 29; 31; 33	concept	13
assignment	11; 21; 28	concluding	14; 21; 31
assistance	27	conclusion	12; 29; 31
assistant	5; 22	conference	4; 30
attraction	7	connecting	8–9
aunt	8	contact	5; 20; 22–23; 29; 31
author	14	contrasting	17; 20
available	3–4 ; 18	cook	8
avoid	8	corporation	32
awake	9	correct	7–9
balanced	8	couple	31
benefit	14; 16; 18; 22; 29; 30	cousin	7–8
bicycle	8	create	12; 19; 32
bold	7–8	creation	32
brain	9	creative	32
bus	8	creativity	32
busy	8	credit	15
challenge	12; 13; 18	cultural	10
chart	1–6; 10; 13; 15–28; 30–32	culture	10; 22; 23
check	7–9	dance	8
clause	23–28	definition	17
coffee	8	designer	12; 32
colleague	27	device	12
comment	21	dinner	8